	DATE DUE		
OCT 1 1 1988			
NOV 1 2 1997			

Hermits and the New Monasticism
A Study of Religious Communities in Western Europe
1000–1150

Hermits and the
New Monasticism

A Study of Religious Communities in
Western Europe 1000–1150

Henrietta Leyser

ST. MARTIN'S PRESS   New York

All rights reserved. For information, write:
St. Martin's Press, Inc., 175 Fifth Avenue, New York, NY 10010
Printed in Hong Kong
Published in the United Kingdom by The Macmillan Press Ltd.
First published in the United States of America in 1984

ISBN 0-312-36999-9

Library of Congress Cataloging in Publication Data

Leyser, Henrietta.
  Hermits and the new monasticism.

  Bibliography: p.
  Includes index.
  1. Hermits – Europe – History. 2. Monasticism and
religious orders – History – Middle Ages, 600–1500.
I. Title.
BX2847.E85L49 1984   271'.02'094   83–40611
ISBN 0-312-36999-9

FOR KARL

Contents

Acknowledgements

THIS book was originally written as a B. Litt. thesis in the early 1960s. In attempting to patch and mend it so many years later I am painfully aware how threadbare it still is. I owe a great deal to many friends. I hope they will forgive me if I mention here only my first tutor, Beryl Smalley, my supervisor, Richard Southern, who first suggested the subject to me, and both Denis Bethell and Maurice Keen as editors. I would also like to thank the trustees of the William Abel Pantin Memorial Fund for their generosity. My greatest debt is to my family and to their tolerance of 'wilderness'.

Islip
1983   Henrietta Leyser

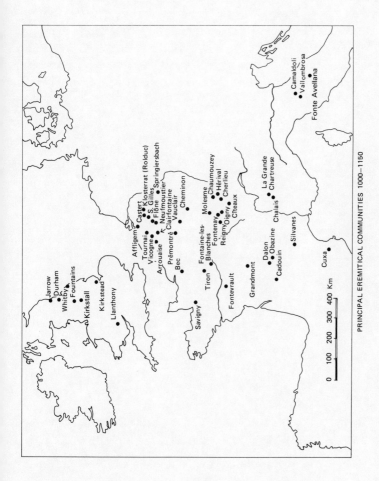

PRINCIPAL EREMITICAL COMMUNITIES 1000—1150

Jarrow
Durham
Whitby
Fountains
Kirkstall
Kirkstead
Llanthony

Affligem Castert
Tournai
Vicogne S. Gilles
Arrouaise
Prémontré Clairfontaine
Bec
Savigny
Tiron
Fontaine-les-Blanches
Fontevrault

Klosterrat (Rolduc)
Flône Springersbach
Neufmoustier
Vauclair
Cheminon
Molesme Chaumouzey
Hérival
Fontenay Cherlieu
Reigny Oigny
Cîteaux
Grandmont
Dalon La Grande
Obazine Chartreuse
Cadouin Chalais
Silvanes
Cuxa
Camaldoli
Vallombrosa
Fonte Avellana

0 100 200 300 400 Km

1. Introduction

the whole world a hermitage
Damian, *Vita Romualdi*

TALKING about hermits provokes mirth; if you do not believe this, try working on hermits and keeping a goat. Like goats, hermits are usually seen as wayward and smelly – just occasionally as romantic but definitely as fringe creatures and in some sense failures, eking out their existence on some unpromising patch of scrub. To quote a recent review in the *Times Literary Supplement* 'the hermit's life, like chicken farming seems to have provided one of the refuges for the human wreckage caused by the first world war'.[1] The perspective of the middle ages was different. Hermits were to be found on the very highest rung of the ladder of perfection. Abbots, kings and emperors would seek their advice. Because it was so exacting a life only those of proven calibre were encouraged to take it up.

The eleventh and twelfth centuries saw a dramatic change: 'it seemed as if the whole world would be turned into a hermitage'.[2] Hermits were everywhere, on every rostrum. They came from all walks of life. Robbers gave up their lives of pillage to become hermits; monks left their communities and masters their schools. Why was this so? First of all, as we shall see, there is a semantic problem. Much confusion could have been avoided if these new hermits of the eleventh and twelfth centuries had presumed to call themselves 'holy men'. Hermits, traditionally, withdraw in ones or twos from the world:

> Living a sane and gentle life in a forest nook or a hill pocket
> Perpetuating their kind and their kindness, keeping
> Their hands clean and their eyes keen, at one with
> Themselves, each other and nature.[3]

They are not expected to try to reform the world, to become wandering preachers, to take upon themselves the care of lepers, prostitutes, the sick and the poor, to proclaim by word and deed that most existing ecclesiastical institutions were at worst rotten, at best inadequate. But this is what the new hermits of the eleventh and twelfth centuries did and throughout Europe they founded communities where they could, in their sense, live perfectly.

Everyone can recognise, in parlour-game terms, 'what the consequence was'. Cluniac monasteries were now challenged by communities proclaiming quite different values and observances. Monastic historians following Ordericus Vitalis have described how 'monasteries are founded everywhere...observing new rites...the swarm of cowled monks spreads all over the world'.[4] In the unforgettable words of David Knowles 'the single traditional version of the monastic life [was split] into twenty different divisions, as it were the colours of the spectrum'.[5] Bitter arguments broke out as to which way of life was best, whose profession the most authentic.

The end of the story, in a sense, came with the pronouncement of the Lateran Council of 1215 forbidding any further new orders, but it is with the beginnings of these developments that we are concerned here. For in most accounts there is a hiatus, a passing over of the crucial years between the first meeting of any hermits (in a forest or a 'desert', clad in scruffy clothes) and the founding of their communities. The improbability that such a meeting of 'marginal' and traditionally solitary figures could lead to such momentous, central monastic changes is felt to be so great, even ludicrous, that barely any attempt has been made to spell out what 'he said to him', or, as was sometimes the case 'to her'. There is, in short, a failure to connect. Hermits and monks are still kept in separate, quite artificial compartments. They are even seen as diametrical figures. Here is a recent example. Brenda Bolton, following Christopher Brooke, writes: 'the hermit life was revived in a world in which its opposite, the communal mode of life, flourished as never before'.[6] For both writers it is the Carthusians who seem to span the poles: but for the eleventh and twelfth centuries this contrast between the eremitical and the communal life is false. Certainly, as we shall see, there were still solitaries – these I have called 'traditional hermits' – but there were also 'new hermits' for whom solitude had an entirely different meaning. These hermits were the parents of the new orders, of the Cistercians just as much as of the Carthusians, of the Vallombrosans and the Premonstratensians, just as much as of the more isolated Camaldolensians. They saw themselves as hermits and the *Lives* and *Rules* of their communities describe the ways in which they chose to live 'eremitically'. A hermit was no longer a solitary figure in a hut or cave; he belonged, in every sense of the word, to a group of pioneers, to 'le *take-off*[7] of the twelfth century. Ordericus knew this too. In the course of describing the peace Henry I had brought to England he continues: 'hermits can add their testimony, for they cut down dense woods and now give praise in the high-roofed monasteries and spiritual palaces built there chanting glory to God with peace of mind where formerly robbers and outlaws used to hide to perform their evil deeds'.[8]

How the hermits became monks and canons will be considered later; the fundamental question must be 'Why?' According to one school of thought it was because they had no choice: hermits were utopians, utopians never survive, sooner or later they have to face either extermination or assimilation. Another closely related argument is this: the hermits were led at first by men of great charisma, but because of the huge size of their followings charisma was replaced by institutions. The hermits adopted rules and orders because they had to, but this transition was also an act of treason. By becoming monks and canons the hermits were admitting to compromise and failure.

There can be no doubt that there are details in these arguments which must be accepted. At first, the hermits did obey leaders, not rules. Then, 'small is beautiful' – for any community success creates problems. Here, as an example, is the weary lament of a twelfth-century prior whose house had once contained only seven brethren: 'the number of the religious grows, and at the same time trouble increases; being a large number they need many goods, and many goods not only cause discord between religious and seculars, but also among religious themselves....what was before given freely, must now be bought, and the property that was peacefully owned can now scarcely be kept without a law-suit'.[9] It is clear that the hermits themselves were often far from pleased with the outcome of their ventures; they might even leave their first foundations and try again. But the point that must be made is this: the unwieldly size of many hermitages caused problems, but not rules. Rules to the hermits were not a sign of failure, but 'structures for....piety',[10] the embodiment of their ideals.

The renaissance of the twelfth century was (among other things) a search for new forms. Giles Constable has shown how its vocabulary reflects this preoccupation: recreate, remake, restore, repair, regenerate, reflower, rekindle, revive, resuscitate, these are only some of the words that continually occur. 'Behold matter', wrote Bernard Silvester, 'the oldest thing [in creation], wishes to be born again and in this new beginning to be encompassed in forms.'[11] By the end of the century, according to Constable, there had been a shift from 'what may be called a backward-looking to a forward-looking ideology of reform'.[12] The 'forward-looking' ideology will lead to apocalyptic schools of thought, the 'backward-looking' school takes us straight to the hermits. It was their yearning for models from Scripture and the early Fathers which shaped and moulded their lives, which gave urgency to their search for rules. The cry for a return to the perfection of earlier norms can be heard persistently from the time of Romuald's wanderings in Spain and Italy through to the heyday of Cistercianism: 'to put all in brief no perfection expressed in the words of the Gospel, or of the apostles, or in the writings of the Fathers, or in the saying of the monks of old is wanting to our order and our way of life'.[13]

The Cistercians' rule must be the most thumbed of all the statutes to which the hermit-movement gave birth. The organisation it set up has been described by Richard Southern as 'a masterpiece of medieval planning', successful, partly, because of its attention to detail; 'pigs', for example, 'though they wander by day must return to the styes at night'.[14] One is reminded of the similar efficiency shown by William I in the compiling of Domesday: 'there was not.... – it is shameful to record it, but it did not seem shameful for him to do it – not even one ox, nor one cow, nor one pig which escaped notice in his survey'.[15] This is not fortuitous. One of the characteristics of the eleventh and twelfth centuries was this new respect for the written word, for the value of legal precision and codification; the great achievement of the hermits and their followers was the ability to combine this legalism, this concern with outward forms, with an equally intense scrutiny of inner feeling.

The search for new forms of monasticism is always, as M. Séguy has said, the search for a new society. This is no place to examine the fundamental changes, social and economic, of twelfth-century Europe. On the other hand it was precisely these developments which dictated the pace and direction of the spiritual 'renewing of structures'.[16] It was economic expansion and social change which made the hermit movement both possible and necessary.

From the mid-eleventh century Europe was free from external attack. The pagan invaders of the tenth century had in turn been repelled and converted. But the relative peace that was to follow brought its own turmoil, more devastating, more irreparable, than the sporadic acts of pillage. The tenth century had known a certain grim security. Communities were small, self-contained, purposeful. What mattered was survival, either in this world or the next, but this was a struggle that was shared and reliably supported on many levels, by the company of saints and kinsmen and of monks at prayer. The eleventh century brought changes which shattered this pattern of existence. They have been much discussed: the great increase in population, improved agricultural techniques, rural dislocation, the growth of towns and the schools and, above all, the spread of a money economy:

> Money! He's the whole world's master
> His the voice that makes men run:
> Speak! Be quiet! Slower! Faster!
> Money orders – and it's done.[17]

The hermit movement has sometimes been seen as a simple turning away from these new developments, as a 'rejection of both the new cities and the old monasteries'.[18] Certainly it is true that the hermits hated both cities and money, conversely that they wanted to live as poor men in the 'desert'. But the movement should not be seen in this purely negative fashion. The 'desert' was not a sandy place where the hermits could bury their heads; they went there, as had their Lord, to 'find themselves', to consider how to meet the new challenge, how to find a form of living that would be appropriate, as Cluniac monasticism no longer was, to their circumstances and their aspirations.

The desert, as Isaiah had seen it, was 'the place of future renewal': 'the desert shall rejoice and blossom as the rose. It shall blossom abundantly and rejoice even with joy and singing' (Isaiah xxxv, 1–2). Gregorian reform, according to Janet Nelson: '[by] involving a new degree of religious differentiation within the wider social system, and a revaluation of religious commitments for all adherents was the answer to newly-felt demands'.[19] In support, she cites Anselm and Damian. Anselm, as we know from his *Life*, seriously considered becoming a hermit, Peter Damian was the great propagator of the movement. This is no coincidence. There can be no doubt that it was above all the hermits in the eleventh and twelfth centuries who were asking not just for themselves but for all Western Christendom, 'what good must I do to win eternal life?' For too long the answers of key figures have dominated historical thinking: the answers, however controversial, of Gregory VII himself, of St Bernard, of Abelard. It is time to see what answers the hermits gave and how deeply their response permeates all the new religious structures of the eleventh and twelfth century. But first we must look at the traditional background from which the hermits stepped.

2. The Shaping of Tradition

The Flight to the Desert, 250–550

MONASTICISM begins with hermits: in the third and fourth centuries in Egypt and in Syria Christians fled from their towns and villages to remote parts of the countryside, to the deserts of Pispir and of Nitria, to the mouths of the Nile and the Euphrates. In the first place, they may have fled to avoid imperial persecution; when this ceased, shortly after the conversion of Constantine in 312, it is more difficult to suggest any single reason for their flight but it would seem that they wanted then to escape a world which had become too ready to accept them, a world in which they felt that Christians had forgotten the example of Christ and the teaching of the Gospels. For they did not imagine that they had gone to the desert to create a new way of life or to follow any new standard of perfection. Their one aim was to lead the full Christian life, apart from society only because it was not possible to do so within it.

Of the early desert Christians the most celebrated by contemporaries and by later monks was St Antony (c.251–356). His *Life* written (almost certainly) by Athanasius, bishop of Alexandria (328–73) was widely read in the East and in the West and it was through it that he came to be honoured both as the first hermit and as the founder of monasticism. Antony, according to Athanasius, had left the world at the age of twenty and for the next twenty years he lived in complete seclusion in a ruined fortress. When he emerged he had mastered both the devil and his own passions. This gave him the right, even the obligation to lead: 'he persuaded many to embrace the solitary life and thus monasteries were built in the mountains and the desert was filled with monks, with men who having renounced all their goods had dedicated themselves to the eternal city'.[1]

Antony's followers settled throughout Northern Egypt. Their life was predominantly eremitical, that is to say they lived as hermits in cells, alone or with one or two companions, but at times they came together as a community. In Nitria, for example, there was a centre with a church, a guest house and a bakery. Every Saturday and Sun-

7

day the hermits met there, ate and worshipped together. They brought with them whatever they had made in their cells during the week, such as baskets. They were given materials for further work and they received their weekly portion of bread. There was the minimum of formal organisation: asceticism was maintained not by rules but by rivalry.

The freedom of this form of life has been taken as an explanation of coenobitism, of full community life: '...the hermits were a clear menace to orderly Christian society. Each of them organised his life on his own lines, defying the authority of the bishops and claiming to be the embodiment of the perfect Christian... A solution of the dilemma was found in creating monastic orders where collective life according to strictly ascetic rules replaced the hermit's individual escape from this world'.[2] This is too rationalised an approach. Pachomius, who founded the first known coenobitical community at Tabennisi on the right bank of the Nile c.315, was not the successor of St Antony, but his contemporary. He too lived for a time as a hermit and then felt he must become a leader but unlike Antony he was interested not only in the guidance but also in the organisation of his disciples and he wrote for them the earliest extant monastic rule. His monks were divided into houses and were subject first to the superior of their house, and ultimately to the superior of the monastery. They met twice a day to eat and three times for prayer. Much of the day was spent in manual labour which was organised with self-sufficiency as its aim, each house having its own particular craft.

There were then, by 350, at least two distinct forms of the religious life, the eremitical and the coenobitical; it was left to St Basil to judge between them. He chose the latter. After spending a year visiting monks in Egypt, Syria, Mesopotomia and Palestine, Basil returned to his home near Neo-Caesarea where, in 358, he founded his own community. The eremitical life he rejected for two reasons. Solitude was dangerous: 'One who lives in isolation will not easily discover his own failings since he has no-one to reprove or correct him gently and kindly. His is the fate spoken of in Ecclesiastes iv. 10: "Woe to him that is alone! For, if he falleth, there is none to raise him up".'[3] Secondly, the communal life alone, Basil believed, gave scope for the exercise of the Christian virtues of humility and charity: '...the Lord...so as to transmit to us clearly and exactly the example of humility in the perfection of charity girded Himself and washed the feet of the disciples. Whom, therefore, will you wash, to whom will you minister, compared to whom will you be the lowest, if you live alone? ... An arena of combat, a good path of progress, a continual discipline, and a practising of the Lord's commandments: all this is the dwelling together of brethren in a community.'[4]

Knowledge of the work of Basil, of Antony and of Pachomius was quickly transmitted to the West. Athanasius, exiled from Alexandria (in his determination to fight heresy he had offended the emperor Constantine) lived in Trier for a year and then in Rome. In 357 his *Life* of Antony appeared; by the third quarter of the century it had been translated from the Greek into Latin. St Jerome in the first decade of the fifth century translated the *Rule of Pachomius*; Rufinus of Aquileia, at about the same time, the *Rules of Basil*. A little later, between 414 and 429 came the work of Cassian who, having lived for fifteen years among the Egyptian hermits, described their beliefs and practices for the monks of Provence. The inflammatory effect these writings could have is well-known from the *Confessions of St Augustine*. St Augustine, on hearing for the first time of St Antony and of those who through reading his *Life* had become monks, was overcome with shame. In turmoil he listened to a voice 'tolle legi, tolle legi' ('Take, read'), and remembering that Antony had been converted by a verse of the Gospel, heard by chance, Augustine opened his copy of St Paul and read the first passage that met his eye, Romans xiii:13,14. This marked the end of his struggles: '...the light of peace seemed to be shed upon my heart and every shadow of doubt melted away'.[5]

Despite his debt to the hermit Antony, Augustine himself came to advocate not the solitary life but the shared experience of coenobitism. For many writers, however, the eremitical life, at least in theory, was supreme. This was the lesson which both Jerome and Cassian had brought from the East and it had local roots in Sulpicius Severus' *Life of St Martin of Tours* (c.363-420/5). But as St Martin himself found, it was not always possible to be a hermit nor, as Jerome and Cassian were anxious to point out, was it always desirable.

Jerome's teaching may be found in a letter to a certain Rusticus, who it is thought later became bishop of Narbonne. It is a long letter on how Rusticus, who has become a monk, should live and it thus covers the problem whether he should in Jerome's words 'be alone or in a monastery with others'. Jerome has no hesitations:

I would prefer you to have the society of holy men and not to be your own teacher. If you set out on a strange road without a guide you may easily at the start take a wrong turning and make a mistake, going too far or not far enough, running till you weary yourself or delaying your journey for a little sleep. In solitude pride quickly creeps in, and when a man has fasted a little while and has seen no-one, he thinks himself a person of some account. He forgets who he is.... he does what he pleases. What then will you say? Do I disapprove of the solitary life? Not at all: I have often commended it, but I wish to see the soldiers who march out of a monastery-school men who have not been frightened by their early training, who have given proof of a holy life for many months...[6]

Cassian's views are more elaborate than Jerome's; common to both, however, is this concept of the monastery as a place of preparation for a hermitage. Cassian's approach is historical. Coenobites he believed to be the 'oldest kind of monk', dating even from the time of the apostles. It was the coenobitical life which the apostles had taught to the first generation of Christians; only when standards within the church had deteriorated was there any need for Christians who wanted to live coenobitically to retreat from society and to form a separate estate. In time the more spiritually advanced members of these communities became hermits: 'from the number of these perfect men (the coenobites) there came forth the fruits and flowers of the anchorites or hermits'.[7] To Cassian, hermits had by definition first been monks, trained for their new vocation in the 'wrestling ground of a monastery'.[8] They were those who, 'formed in monasteries, made perfect in the ascetic life have preferred the secrets of solitude'.[9] But while Cassian does not envisage Jerome's problem of anyone becoming a hermit before he has been a monk he does discuss the related question of monks who have become hermits too soon. On the one hand, there are those who have deluded themselves in thinking that they are ready to leave their houses; these in fact 'do not even know why solitude is desirable and must be sought ... they imagine that the whole virtue of their way of life consists only in avoiding the company of their brethren...'[10] But there had also appeared in recent years a yet worse type of hermit who had retired to solitude because he had neither the humility nor the patience to stay in his monastery any longer. For this kind of hermit perfection would never be possible. Not only would his vices remain uncorrected, they would also become more grave.

The nature of the ideal eremitical life is also discussed by Cassian. He gives what was to become the accepted reason for its superiority over the coenobitic, that is, that it is the more contemplative. 'The perfection of the hermit lies in his having freed himself from all earthly concerns, and in as far as his human frailty allows, of uniting himself thus with Christ.'[11] The hermit's life is the accomplishment of the third abnegation: a Christian might first renounce the riches and gains of the world, then all evil thoughts and passions and finally he might give up all things present and visible to contemplate only those that were to come. This was the eremitical life, 'spiritual purity',[12] a state which the coenobite only rarely attained.

The eremitical and the coenobitical life were thus, according to the teaching of both Jerome and Cassian, not so much alternative forms of the religious life but rather different stages of it. The corollary of this, that it should be the aim of every monk to become a hermit does, moreover, seem to have been put into practice. At Vivarium, a house founded in the sixth century by the Roman senator Cassiodorus, there was a recognised place of retreat for those monks who wanted to be hermits:

> If as is likely, God's grace assisting, you be adequately instructed by the discipline of the monastery and it happens that your purified minds require something more sublime, then you have the sweet recesses of Mount Castellius, where with God's help you may live happily as anchorites. Wherefore it will be fitting for you when you are disciplined and completely proved to choose that for your dwelling.[13]

Most important for the West was that St Benedict shared this view. His teaching on the subject is less compact than Cassiodorus' but it may be pieced together from the opening and the conclusion of his *Rule*. In his general discussion on monks Benedict follows Cassian very closely. There are, he wrote, four kinds of monks, Coenobites and Hermits, Sarabaites and Gyrovagues. The first two he admires, the last two he finds detestable because of their self-indulgence and lack of discipline. Sarabaites are those 'who not having been tested, as gold in the furnace, by any rule or by the lessons of experience, are as soft and yielding as lead'.[14] In contrast to these the Coenobites are 'a strong race',[15] yet Benedict calls his own only 'beginners'[16] in the religious life. His monastery is a 'school of the Lord's service'[17] but his rule will teach no more than 'some degree of virtue and the rudiments of monastic observance';[18] the 'perfection of the monastic life'[19] is outside its scope. It is clearly this perfection which hermits seek for they are described as 'those who not in the first fervour of their conversion but after long probation in a monastery ... go out well-armed ... to the solitary combat of the desert'.[20] It is indeed probable that there were at Monte Cassino, as at Vivarium, special arrangements for those who wanted to become hermits; it is also likely that Benedict himself never fully participated in the communal life of his foundations and that he thus preferred, and ultimately wanted his disciples to prefer, the life of a hermit.

Monks and Hermits, 550–1150

FROM 550–1150 the views of Benedict and Cassian on the superiority of the hermit's life were accepted and repeated, but they were also modified. Above all it was the dangers of the eremitical life which were stressed so that it became exceptional rather than usual for monks to become hermits. It was pointed out, time and again, that special gifts were needed to be a hermit, that it was not a suitable life for everyone and that to undertake it without the necessary vocation could be disastrous. Smaragdus, the Carolingian abbot, in his commentary on the *Rule of Benedict* quoted for the first chapter Cassian's words that hermits and anchorites were 'the fruits and flowers' [21] of coenobitism but all the same concluded with a verdict in favour of coenobites: 'the solitary is faced with many dangers...therefore it is better to be a monk in a monastery'.[22] Grimlaicus, the author of a ninth/tenth-century rule for solitaries gave this warning: 'to enter the solitary life is the highest perfection; to live imperfectly is to incur the greatest damnation'.[23]

There was, nonetheless, no lack of hermits throughout the whole of this period; the evidence for their existence may be varied and scattered but it is also constant. Chroniclers of monastic houses with which they had connections have recorded their fame, both in annals and in full-scale *Lives*, and recalled their asceticism; archaeological discoveries have given some idea of the kind of cells in which they lived and the sites they chose; conciliar decrees show how attempts were made to exercise some control over their entry into the eremitical life and their subsequent activities. These sources, taken together, show hallmarks which did not change greatly from one century to another: hermits live alone or with, at the most, one or two companions. Their lives are simpler, more austere and more contemplative than those of other religious. It is therefore they, above all, who deserve to be called the true philosophers of Christ. In this there is little that could not be found already in the description of Gregory of Tours (c.540–94) of the hermit with his garden, accompanied by beasts and birds, dedicated to a life of prayer and fasting, from which nothing could distract him since 'except for God he had nothing'.[24] However, it is important to understand that precisely because of the seeming simplicity of his life the hermit might often become caught up in the complexities of others – his 'apartness' gave him a special ability to solve 'the common troubles of mankind'.[25] Like the holy man of Late Antiquity, as defined by Peter Brown, he was 'the bearer of objectivity in society'.[26] Henry Mayr-Harting has shown how this definition still rings true for twelfth-century England. Wulfric, recluse of Haselbury Plucknett, Somerset, was a highly respected therapist who could 'fulfil many needs, resolve many tensions'.[27]

The reasons for becoming a hermit have always been many, the need for a life of greater contemplation by no means the only motive. In the early middle ages a hermitage might be a respectable refuge for those who, in differing ways, did not conform to the mould of an increasingly institutionalised monasticism. There were scholars, such as Hrabanus Maurus, former abbot of Fulda (d.856) for whom the eremitical life gave more time for intellectual work; there were laymen who, because of their illiteracy, felt themselves unable to participate adequately in communal life. Wulsi of Evesham, for example, a layman who was professed at Crowland in the eleventh century, found himself ill at ease in both the liturgical and administrative activities of the community. His prior was sympathetic and he was allowed to leave Crowland and to become a hermit in a cave near Evesham. For women, the eremitical life might offer escape from parental marriage plans. It was not easy to be accepted as a nun without the consent of parents but it was sometimes possible to flee to a hermitage. Christina of Markyate, for example, a noble-woman of Anglo-Saxon ancestry of the early twelfth century, forced into marriage by persistent parents, was helped to run away and become a recluse by the network of hermits who lived in her neighbourhood. It is also worth noticing in connection with Christina how to be a hermit could have a political connotation. Christina's hermit-friends were, as she was, of Anglo-Saxon stock, 'ministering to a people who were not at home with the Anglo-Norman culture'.[28]

Christina's chosen vocation, to be a recluse, was the most rigorous form of the eremitical life possible. Strictly speaking, although circumstances could alter cases, the recluse, once immured, was never allowed to leave his cell. This, which appears as one of the conditions of Grimlaicus's *Rule* of the ninth century was graphically illustrated by the use of the Office of the Dead when a recluse was immured and by the tales of chroniclers of recluses who had preferred to die by fire and by the sword rather than to move from their cells. But to be a recluse was not to be cut off from all human contact. Grimlaicus himself suggested that recluses should live with two or three others nearby, that their cells should be adjacent to a church so that they could participate in the services and that they should be hospitable to the poor. A recluse might also live with or near a disciple who was destined to succeed him in his cell. He would probably have a servant and he might (like Wulfric of Haselbury) attract many visitors seeking his advice.

At the other end of the scale from the recluse were 'part-time' hermits, that is, bishops and abbots who had eremitical retreats as a kind of sabbatical leave. St Anskar, for example, when he became archbishop of Bremen in about 848, had a cell built for himself 'so that he might practise divine philosophy'.[29] Closely associated with this was the custom whereby an abbot might become a hermit on retirement. The eremitical life was both a rest from and a reward for administrative services. An abbot might make use of both practices. Hermenland, the first abbot of Aindre, an eighth-century foundation, always spent Lent in solitude; then, when he became old and found the position too great a burden, he resigned and spent the rest of his life as a hermit. This last step had its own conventions, it was not something that could be anticipated. Medericus, abbot of Autun in the late seventh century, wanted to become a hermit 'since he did not feel that he could gain the highest reward among so many people ... [and he therefore] looked for a deserted place'.[30] The brethren of his house had him recalled on the grounds that he could do greater good by his example and it was not until the end of his life that he was finally able to leave his post to become a hermit.

A monk who wanted to become a hermit might also have difficulty in obtaining, in this case from his abbot, the necessary permission.

An abbot might be afraid that the monk had not yet proved himself and that his wish to become a hermit reflected only a desire for change. On the other hand, the monk might be a well-trusted figure in the community whose help the abbot was reluctant to lose. In one such case it was St Benedict himself who is said to have appeared to the abbot and to have told him to release the monk. Once permission had been granted there is no evidence of further conflict or difficulty. The hermits often chose to live on monastic land and even to remain under the jurisdiction of their former abbots. Roger, the protector of Christina of Markyate, was described by the monk of St Alban's who wrote her *Life* as 'a monk of ours [who] lived in a hermitage, though even here he kept obedience to his abbot'.[31] In these cases the monks seem to have been proud of their hermits. Monks from Reichenau used to visit their hermit, Meinrad (d.861) and spend the night in his cell. At Fontenelle, a vine planted by the hermit Milo 'while he was philosophising'[32] was one of the exhibits of the house. A monastery might also take under its protection lay hermits who had never been professed as monks, who wanted some guidance in the solitary life and who also needed to be able to share in the sacramental life of a community since they themselves could not say Mass. Cluny, for example, had from the time of her foundation a hermit, Adhegrinus, once a companion of Odo's, who remained a hermit when Odo joined Baume and later followed him to Cluny. He used to come to the monastic church on Sundays and feast days and on these occasions he collected his food – a little flour with which to make bread and a few beans. In England, the famous Godric of Finchale (d.1170) put himself under the spiritual direction of the prior of Durham.

This peaceful co-existence between monks and hermits was possible only because it had become the belief that the eremitical life was the way for the few. It might be the eccentric, the poor, the unlearned, or the distinguished who became hermits; it was not the lot of the ordinary monk. Coenobites had therefore no reason to feel that the greater asceticism of the hermits was a reproach against their own more moderate lives and there is nothing to suggest that the hermits ever tried to win over monks to the eremitical life. But there appeared in the eleventh and twelfth centuries a new kind of hermit, very different in character from the traditional hermit. He was militant and aggressive, he attacked established forms of monasticism and he thereby provoked a 'crisis of coenobitism'.[33]

The most paradoxical characteristic of the new hermits was that they formed communities and became in time monks or canons. The Benedictine definition of a hermit was thus reversed: it was no longer monks who became hermits but rather hermits who became monks. It could, however, be argued that this had sometimes happened in the ninth and tenth centuries and that all that was new in the eleventh and twelfth century was the scale on which it occurred; what had before happened only rarely, then became common. Before examining the ideas and activities of the hermits of the eleventh and twelfth century something must be said of those who, at first glance, might seem to be their forefathers.

The first of these is Benedict of Aniane. Benedict in 774 became a monk at the house of St Seine-l'Abbaye. From the start he imposed on himself a much severer regime than the *Rule of Benedict* required. The *Rule of Benedict*, he claimed, was intended only for beginners. Those who were more advanced should try to follow the rules of Basil and of Pachomius. On being elected abbot Benedict declined and indeed left St Seine-l'Abbaye altogether. He returned to his own estates and there built himself a cell in which he lived for some time as a hermit. Disciples gathered around him and Benedict soon began to organise a community with particularly ascetic rules. Vineyards, sheep, horses and serfs were refused; there were to be no silver vessels for the altar, no silk chasubles.

In the tenth century came the reforms of John of Gorze and of Odo of Cluny. John of Gorze wanted to become a monk but because he could find no house where the *Rule* seemed to him to be properly kept he went instead to live with certain hermits around Metz. He made a pilgrimage to Rome and was impressed by the communities of Benevento which lived by manual labour and which he would have liked to imitate. Odo of Cluny too was a hermit before he went to Baume since he and his companion Adhegrinus 'could find no religious house in which they felt inclined to remain'.[34]

These episodes are indeed similar to those in the *Lives* of the new hermits of the eleventh and twelfth centuries; but they were, and this was the great difference, no more than episodes. Benedict of Aniane's final contribution to monasticism represented not a development from his experiences as a hermit but rather a rejection of them. For reasons which can only be guessed Benedict deliberately turned away from his eremitical, individualistic aspirations. His customs demanded observance of the Benedictine rule but both allowed and encouraged concessions, placed to the fore not manual labour but the liturgy. These customs, ratified at the Council of Aachen in 817, were to be binding on all monks within the Carolingian Empire and it was on them that the later work of both Odo of Cluny and John of Gorze was founded. Like Benedict they too abandoned any concept they may once have had of a more austere form of the monastic life. The elaborate liturgy favoured by these reformers made it physically impossible for monks to work in the fields, as St Benedict had envisaged, and theoretically irrelevant. The role of the monk in tenth-century Europe was to pray for the well-being of Christian kingdoms and their rulers and the defeat of their enemies. The monk was a spiritual warrior, fighting not only for the salvation of his soul but also for the prosperity of society. Monasticism was no longer 'a flight into desert places undertaken by individuals under the stress of a strong conviction; it was the expression of the corporate religious ideals and needs of a whole community'.[35]

3. The New Hermits

IN 1925 a study by Alice Cooke of twelfth-century religious revival and reform made no mention at all of hermits. Three years later came the publication by Dom Morin of Rainaud the hermit's letters to Ivo of Chartres attacking contemporary monasticism, an episode, as Morin called it, in 'the crisis of coenobitism'. Morin himself might have been surprised if he could have foreseen how often the phrase would be used. It did not seem to him a moment of particular significance. Rainaud the hermit was something of a hothead, not a very reasonable man:

> Certainly the monastic order of the twelfth century showed signs of decadence and this, no doubt, was one of the causes which led to renewed enthusiasm for the solitary life, represented particularly in the north-west of France by Robert of Arbrissel, Vitalis of Mortain, William Firmat and the great crowd of their disciples...but this was only a fleeting episode in the history of western asceticism and the results were nothing compared with those of the great monastic orders already in existence.[1]

Morin's judgement must be compared with that of Dom Jean Leclercq summing up the work of a conference on hermits held at La Mendola in 1962:

> Eremitism exercised an influence direct or indirect on every manifestation of spiritual life, indeed in many areas of the life of the church...in the religious movements of the period eremitism does not perhaps explain everything, yet there is hardly anything that can be completely understood without it.[2]

Between these two views of the eremitical life, whether it be peripheral or central, lie over thirty years of research into many of the new communities of the eleventh and twelfth centuries. Gradually it has become evident how many of these foundations were eremitical in origin; to quote Leclercq again: 'one can talk of monastic, canonical, clerical, missionary, pilgrim, hospitaller, lay, military [and] crusading eremitism'.[3] But if this is so, if the hermit has become such a chameleon, how can one possibly recognise him? A new definition for this particular kind of hermit is necessary and a few fallacies, old and new, must be exposed.

In the first place, it must not be supposed that the eremitical movement of the eleventh and twelfth centuries meant simply more hermits of every kind, sharing in a revived love of the solitary life. This is how the movement used to be interpreted and echoes of this interpretation may still be found. For a classic statement of the case one may turn to Leclercq and Bonnes' study of John of Fécamp (1946) where 'the prestige which the eremitical life was beginning to enjoy' in the early eleventh century was illustrated by citing Richard of St Vannes, St Romuald, St Bruno, Adhegrinus of Cluny and the hermits who later settled near Cluny as examples of the 'new tendency'.[4] But it is in fact only the lives of Bruno and Romuald which show new perspectives. The others were following well-known and well-worn forms of the eremitical life: Richard, the abbot tired of his administrative duties, Adhegrinus the recluse unattracted by any form of community life, the hermits near Cluny examples of those monks who, in the words of the Benedictine rule, were 'not in the first fervour of their conversion, but after long probation, in a monastery...[had gone] out..to the solitary combat of the desert'.[5] To place them beside Romuald and Bruno who, by their foundations, brought a new and original meaning to eremitism is to blur and even to lose sight of the distinctive character of the eremitical movement. Although the new hermits of this movement had some of the same observances as the traditional hermits their aims and their outlook were different, even in some respects antagonistic. The ideals of a Richard of St Vannes were not theirs; on the contrary, he was a representative of the monasticism they rejected as corrupted and debased. Their first spokesman, Peter Damian, recalled a dream of St Richard in purgatory expiating his love of fine buildings.

The first difference between the new and the traditional hermit lies in the very trait they might seem to have in common, love of solitude. The new hermits chose sites far from any habitation, 'deserts', 'wildernesses' in the same way as traditional hermits. St Norbert, for example, is reported as saying 'I have no wish to stay in towns, but rather somewhere wild and remote'.[6] But unlike traditional hermits the new hermits both expected and welcomed companions; solitude did not mean for them to be without the company of fellow religious but to be apart from secular society, from 'the bustle of everyday existence',[7] not to be involved in litigation, in buying and selling, not to live 'where the shouts of young men and the singing of girls could be heard'.[8] It seldom meant living alone or the complete absence of community life. Some, like the Carthusians, 'combined solitude with communal life';[9] others, for example the hermits of Camaldoli and Fonte Avellana, followed the traditional Benedictine practice of allowing those who wished for greater seclusion than the community provided to live apart as recluses. At Obazine, an eremitical foundation in Limousin, on the other hand, solitary confinement was the most dreadful punishment the leader, Stephen, could think of (he had found a disciple hoarding money). At Grandmont, the rule allowed for the possibility of a traditional hermit wanting to join the foundation; but it also made it quite clear that he could not come still expecting to live as a solitary. The degrees of personal solitude within the movement thus varied according to the foundation and, to some extent, according to the wishes of the individual. Personal solitude was not, for the new hermits, as it was for the traditional hermit, an essential characteristic of their lives but something not all found either desirable or necessary. What did matter was that the communities, founded in 'forests and deserts' should be cut off and isolated from the world.

For a hermit not to be a solitary is sufficiently unexpected to lead to confusion and misjudgement. For example, merely on this basis historians have argued that neither John Gualbert's foundation of Vallombrosa nor Stephen Harding's of Cîteaux could have been eremitic in character since both were coenobitical and the foundations must be therefore primarily reactions to, rather than part of, the eremitical movement. Other historians talk sometimes of hermits and reforming monks as if they must be distinct and belong to separate camps when they are in fact the same people. Here, for example, is a recent summary:

> Attractive as the revived monasticism of the eleventh and twelfth centuries was for many, it failed to attract others. Hermits, wandering preachers, individual spiritual leaders like Robert of Arbrissel and others appear in greater numbers in the eleventh century.[10]

But was not Robert of Arbrissel, the hermit, also the founder of the monastery of Fontrevault, and, to name but one other, St Norbert, the wandering preacher, the founder of the order of Premonstratensians?

To return to the problem of definitions: if a hermit is not necessarily a solitary who is he? If he did not particularly want to be alone, what then did he seek? Let us hear the hermits themselves. This is how the prologue to the customs of Oigny, a house of hermit canons in Autun, begins:

> By the grace of God we propose to follow the rule of blessed Augustine and the eremitical life: we will follow the rule in all that pertains to the common life so that we will eat, sleep, work and perform the service of God together ... we will live as hermits in all that concerns rigorous abstinence and the total renunciation of secular concerns.[11]

Stephen of Obazine's biographer wrote about the blend in his community of the eremitical and canonical life this description and explanation:

> Receiving whatever was of God and rejecting whatever was of the world, they lived according to the canonical rule as far as the offices were concerned but in principle they lived as hermits. For although canons sing regularly to God, they eat too well, have no lasting silence and do little or no manual work.[12]

The new hermits were concerned primarily with asceticism and austerity and they had not become hermits just because they would not or could not live in a community. Nor do they seem to have become hermits for quite the same grim reasons frequently given in the *Lives* of the traditional hermits, of fighting the devil single-handed, meeting him face to face in solitude. Their biographers certainly recalled their temptations and trials (visitations from vultures and Ethiopians), but it was not these struggles alone which coloured their lives. The eremitical leaders themselves wrote of something different and more positive. Bruno of Chartreuse, for example, writing from Calabria, described the natural beauty of his hermitage and then continued 'only those who have experienced it can know what heavenly joy and benefit the silence and solitude of the desert can bring to those who love it'.[13] To Peter Damian, 'a hermitage is a garden of heavenly delights ... the scent of virtues fills the air with fragrance'.[14]

With this lyricism went also a strictly practical desire to live according to a rule, a wish for an objective standard. It was not the intention of the new hermits to live in communities that were less closely organised or disciplined than those already established. They were not anarchists, and they did not want only pastoral idylls. They sought anxiously for rules that would give their foundations permanence, the chance to obtain 'the divine reward for obedience'[15] and which would prevent their being led astray by 'the spirit of error'.[16]

The hermits' search for rules for their communities will be looked at more closely in a later chapter, but here it must be noticed how it highlights a difference between new and traditional hermits. For traditional hermits the eremitical life was a goal, a definitive state, very probably reached after some previous religious experience. For the new hermits, by contrast, it was not an end but a beginning. While it did not immediately provide them with the security they ultimately wanted of a rule, this was also the reason for its attraction. It gave the hermits the chance they wanted to experiment, to try to formulate their ideals before giving them the force of law. Their period in the desert was a time of training. Thus Ordericus Vitalis wrote of Vitalis of Savigny that he

> determined on putting aside the burdens of worldly cares and riches, to bear the easy yoke of Christ in the footsteps of the apostles and lived for sometime in the wildnerness with a few monks. There he conquered the habits belonging to the easier life he had known before and learnt the discipline of a strict observance. Finally he discovered the village of Savigny ... and began to establish a monastery.[17]

The beginning of a new hermit's career was often, in traditional terms, as strange as its conclusion. The hermits appeared to feel a deep revulsion, either from secular society, or from the life of their monastery which they conceived as too lax. They were not, however, always at all sure how to express their dissatisfaction and their final decision to become hermits might be taken only at random and because no better alternative presented itself. Those who already belonged to a religious community might try first to reform it; such an attempt was made, for example, by St Romuald at St Apollinare in Classe. Those who came straight from the world, on the other hand, often considered first joining some established house and would indeed have done so had they found any they thought suitable.

Stephen of Obazine's biographer explains how Stephen and his companion travelled many miles in search of a religious establishment where they might serve God, but since 'there was not then any sufficiently holy order in those regions'[18] they relinquished the attempt and settled instead at Obazine. The *Life* of Herluin of Bec, too, makes it clear how monasteries might not live up to expectations. Herluin was already thirty-seven when he decided to leave the world. He was at the time in the household of the Count of Brionne, uncertain as to the form his new life should take – 'where to go and how to live'[19] – and because of the condition of the church in Normandy unlikely (according to his biographer) to find anyone who could help him. Once released from the Count's service, he retired to his own land at Bonneville and from there he visited nearby monasteries so that he could try to learn how monks lived. So far from giving him inspiration or instruction what he saw filled him with such dismay that it was only the sight of one monk at prayer that saved him from despair.

For the many, like Herluin, who after their conversion were uncertain of their plans, a common solution was to set off on a journey, or pilgrimage. In general, the hermit's pilgrimage was much less limited in scope than the conventional pilgrimage. It might include visits to shrines, but this was not its main aim. It derived its character not from any specific objective but from the principle of renunciation. The pilgrims had to say farewell to their kin and their homeland and to make themselves exiles in foreign regions; this self-imposed banishment was intended to mirror the fate of humanity in exile from the kingdom of heaven. This spiritual roaming had been a special feature of early Irish christianity but it had come to be accepted on the continent that it was not on the whole suitable for monks who were to remember their vows of stability. The Irish, too, came to see that a love of journeying might be the work of the devil; thus St Comgall may be found expelling the devil from the shoe of a certain Mochuda since he had been making it impossible for Mochuda to spend more than two nights in the same place. For the new hermits, on the other hand, subject as yet to no vows, the unlimited potential of a wandering pilgrimage was ideal. At one and the same time it was a means of atoning for past sins, an opportunity for officially beginning a new way of life, a chance for orientation and reflection. So much can clearly be seen from the experience of the hermit Pons de Léras.

Pons, later the founder of a religious house at Silvanes in Rodez, was for many years, according to his biographer, a cruel and rapacious bandit. After his conversion he not only made restitution to those he had wronged but he also had a list of his sins read out, at his own request, to the faithful assembled for a Palm Sunday Mass and, wearing nothing but a convict's wooden collar, he had himself flagellated before them. It has been suggested that such flagellation stems from Pauline theology, from 'a careful reading of Ephesians'[20] but it makes more sense to place it in a wider context. 'Humbling, stripping and pain', in the words of the anthropologist V. W. Turner are the hallmarks of a life-crisis rite, of liminality, the crossing from one station to another, in which the neophytes must be 'reduced or ground down to a uniform condition to be fashioned anew and endowed with additional powers to enable them to cope with their new station in life'. The chief-elect of the Ndembu, just as the Christian Pons, has to be reviled and beaten, insulted and accused, in a ritual setting which manages to combine, in the same way as the service of Palm Sunday, 'lowliness and sacredness'.[21]

Pons' subsequent travels took him and his companions to many places, Mont-St-Michel, Tours and Compostella among others. According to his biographer:

> throughout their journey they took special care to visit holy places, to seek out religious men everywhere, to ask for the support of their prayers, to learn in which way of life they might thereafter for all time blamelessly serve the Lord.[22]

The archbishop of St James, in particular, recommended that Pons become a hermit, advice which Pons took. Other pilgrims whose journeys ended similarly include the already mentioned Stephen of Obazine and two clerks from the chapel of William the Conqueror, Conon and Heldemar. Conon and Heldemar had left England on the accession of William Rufus, they happened in the course of their wanderings to meet a layman living as a hermit at Tronc Berengar in Arras and they decided to join him. This was the beginning of the congregation of Arrouaise.

The example of Greek monasticism has been suggested as a less accidental, even as a vital factor in making men hermits. It is indisputable that there were in the tenth and eleventh centuries a number of Greek hermits not only in Italy (especially in the South) but also throughout Western Europe and that their asceticism, their practice of manual labour are traits which the new hermits could have borrowed from them. But there is little direct or conclusive evidence that they did (just as there is nothing to prove that early eleventh-century heresy was anything but autochthonous). It is known that Richard of St Vannes and Desiderius of Monte Cassino were influenced by the Greeks, but neither of them were new hermits. Of these, only Stephen of Grandmont acknowledges a debt to the Greeks, to the hermits of Calabria of whom he had learnt while living in the household of the archbishop of Benevento. Romuald, the first of the new hermits, because he came from Ravenna might have felt the impact of Greek influence there but, according to his *Life* by Peter Damian he became a hermit because the monks of his house would not keep the *Rule of Benedict* with sufficient strictness, a cry that would be much repeated. Romuald's own 'noviciate' as a hermit he spent first with Marinus who is described as a 'self-taught' hermit, and then in the Pyrenees under the protection of abbot Guarinus of Cuxa. A treatise of William of St Thierry praises the Carthusians for having revived in the West 'the light of the East', but the reference is not to contemporary Greeks, but to the desert monks, to 'that venerable fervour in the religion of Egypt'.[23]

To search for Greek influences is in any case to miss the point. What is arresting about the eremitical movement is its eruption in different times and in different places, the impossibility on the whole of finding links and prototypes. The perplexities of the hermits themselves as to how to organise their disciples came from this lack of example they felt they could follow. They became hermits not to imitate their contemporaries but rather to shun them, because of their conviction that current modes of living were remote from God and the way he had, through Christ and his apostles, shown them how to live.

Two hermits, Bruno, the founder of the Carthusians, and Rainaud, the correspondent of Ivo of Chartres, have left letters describing their conversions. Bruno is reminding his friend Ralph of the vow they had made to leave the world:

> You remember how one day we were together in the garden by Adam's house...we talked for some time about the false lures and perishable riches of the world and of the joys of eternal glory. Then afire with divine love, we promised, vowed, resolved that we would straightaway leave what was transitory and worldly to take hold of the eternal...[24]

Rainaud's letter (of which there are two versions, a short and a long) is combative and aggressive. Rainaud had been a canon, possibly of St Jean des Vignes in Soissons, and he had to justify having left his house. His letter therefore gives reasons why traditional forms of the religious life seemed to the new hermits to have failed and it is one of the most important *pièces justificatives* of the eremitical movement. First, Rainaud replies to Ivo's specific charge on the scandal he may be causing his community by leaving it, but the larger and more interesting part of the letter is Rainaud's accusations against contemporary monasticism and the standards by which he judges it: coenobites are worldly and live too well, are more interested in battles than in psalms. They have no reverence for poverty. Above all, they never attempt to live according to the precepts of the Gospel. This accusation is the key to the eremitical movement:

> When you mentioned the model of the primitive church to which, as you truly say, I wish to cleave, I rejoiced and with all my heart I thank you for your watchful attention, but good father, as scripture testifies and as I have learnt from your own teaching, the model of the primitive church is no more, nor less than the life of the apostles and the disciples shaped by gospel teaching; the life of those to whom it is said 'if any man will take away thy coat, let him have thy cloak also', those who are forbidden not only to resist theft, but also to go to law; those to whom it is said 'be ye perfect as your heavenly father is perfect'...this manner of perfection can, by your own testimony rarely or ever be kept within monasteries and this I reckon is because the poverty which the poor Christ preached is kept out of them as far as possible.[25]

This was the aim of the new hermits, to relive the life of the apostles (the *vita apostolica*), to revive the model of the early church (the *vita primitiva*), to recreate a way of life they felt existing monasticism had obliterated and forgotten: 'to follow the divine scriptures and to have Christ as our leader'.[26]

To think of monasticism as the *vita apostolica* was not new. The idea that the first monks were the apostles themselves and that their example was kept alive by religious living in a community was a concept made familiar to the middle ages by Cassian and St Augustine. But it had come to be a synonym for the monastic life rather than a comment on how it should be led. The eleventh- and twelfth-century hermits (and other reformers) gave the phrase radical and explosive meanings.

The hermits' approach was twofold. In the first place they scrutinised the New Testament anew. The description of the apostles' way of life in Acts iv:32 and Christ's advice to the rich man in Matthew xix:21 underpinned the priority of poverty. Other texts were used, as we shall see, to justify particular observances, for example, manual labour and the practice of preaching. Secondly, in their search for the *vita apostolica* the hermits included not only the lessons of scripture but also of the whole corpus of early Christian literature and of what may be called the primary rules, that is, the *Rule of Benedict* observed to the letter and more amazingly the *Rule of Augustine* 'discovered' in the eleventh century for this purpose, as a gloss on Gospel teaching. The first generations of Christians had, it was felt, faithfully followed the precepts of the Gospels, had expounded and preserved New Testament principles. The *vita apostolica* was therefore, as Rainaud had claimed, conterminous with the *vita primitiva*, the way of life of the early church.

The hermits therefore emulated not only the apostles but also the desert monks; they tried to keep not only the tenets of Christ but also of the Fathers, of Augustine, Jerome, Benedict and Cassian and they coupled these authorities together. At Hérival, an eremitical foundation in Toul, the hermits did manual work 'as the apostles and the early Fathers';[27] at St Mary's in York a group left the abbey so that they could amend their lives 'according to the rule of St. Benedict, yes indeed, according to the truth of the Gospel'.[28] For, as they further explained,

> whatever St. Benedict ordained was altogether established by the Providence of the Holy Spirit, so that nothing can be imagined that is more profitable, more holy, or more blessed. Indeed, the Rule of St. Benedict is an exposition of the whole Gospel, not allegorically but in terms of simple experience and visible works.[29]

The *Rule of Grandmont*, it is true, stated that the hermits must follow only the Gospel, that the *Rules* of Benedict, of Basil and of Augustine were 'the offshoots and not the root of the religious life'[30] but this was an exceptional and unusual view. In several cases it was patristic literature rather than the Gospels which was the hermits' first source of inspiration. At Tournai, it was his reading of Augustine which influenced Odo, master of the cathedral school, to leave the world: as hermits, he and his companions took *The Lives of the Fathers* and Cassian as their models; at about the same time, in England, a monk of Evesham, Aldwin, was reading Bede: moved by the accounts he read there of the glories of the Northumbrian monks he decided to become a hermit on the site of their monasteries and to follow their example of poverty.

This identification of the *vita primitiva* with the *vita apostolica* gave the eremitical movement its diversity and its shape. By it, the hermits had at their disposal a vast body of literature; this was for them both a source of inspiration and a guide to actual observances. For they were concerned not only with the ideology of the early Christians but also with the exact ways in which they had put their ideals into practice. They wanted therefore to keep rules which had preserved, or which would preserve, those practices as faithfully as possible. It is this – a quasi-legalistic, quasi-historical sense – which makes the hermits unlike other evangelicals, which differentiates their movement from Francis' of the following century. Francis never wanted to write a rule; St Norbert gave this lesson to his disciples:

He insisted that without an order and a rule and the Institutes of the Fathers they would not be able to fully observe the apostolic and evangelical commands.[31]

4. The Origins and Development of the Movement: a Geographical Sketch

THE new hermit movement began in Italy in the late tenth century. It is here associated with Romuald and with Peter Damian, with Romuald as the founder and Damian, his biographer, as the spokesman of the movement and a figure of importance in both papal and imperial circles. Of Damian, however, it must be said at once that he cannot strictly be called a hermit of the new type, for although he wrote the rule for Fonte Avellana he did not found, or help to found it, nor did he belong to it in its earliest, formative years. It is, of course, difficult to know the exact extent to which the customs of Fonte Avellana had evolved when Damian joined it, but it is unlikely that Damian in his rule introduced any fundamental innovation. He himself stated that he was merely describing the life already established and it is only in conclusion that he mentions the changes, which are, on the whole, of a traditional character, that he had wanted or felt it wise to make – the building up of the house's material resources and its library, the acquisition of altar ornaments, the erection of a cloister. Above all, Damian does not, in his writings, give any indication that he ever shared the doubts and hesitations of the hermits of the new movement as to how they should organise their lives. The eremitical life was never for him a time of reflection on such a problem; it was in itself the solution, 'the golden path' to God and there was none other 'so straight, so sure, so unimpeded'.[1] It was also, in Damian's experience, an eremitical life that had definite rules, that was already institutionalised. The uncertainties that had faced Romuald and his first companions already seemed quaint. Marinus, for example, with whom Romuald had first lived as a hermit, is described by Damian in his *Life of Romuald* as having had no master in the eremitical life and as singing the psalter in an apparently curious fashion:

> Certainly he sang the whole psalter each day but uninitiated as he was in any rule of the solitary life, as Blessed Romuald would later jokingly recount, often he would leave his cell and together with a disciple would walk up and down the hermitage singing psalms, sometimes twenty under a certain tree, sometimes thirty or forty.[2]

Romuald himself was born in Ravenna in the mid-tenth century to a noble family. As a young man, according to Damian, he followed to all appearances the ways of the world but inwardly was devout and meditative. The turning point in his life came when his father killed a kinsman in a duel. In horror at the deed and at his own connivance – he had been taken along to give his father support – Romuald fled to the monastery of St Apollinare in Classe. He intended to stay the statutory forty days for a homicide but the pressure of a certain monk together with repeated visions of St Apollinare made him decide to take the habit. As a novice he began both to notice and to censure any falling away from the precepts of the rule. The monks, naturally, resented this criticism from a newcomer. Therefore when, after three years, Romuald asked if he could leave the house to live with the hermit Marinus, permission was readily granted.

In 978 both Marinus and Romuald left Italy to go to the monastery of St Michael of Cuxa in the Pyrennees at the invitation of the abbot Guarinus. With them went the doge of Venice who wanted to flee from the office he had wrongly gained, and a friend of the doge. A hermitage was established on land belonging to Cuxa and Romuald was accepted as leader even by Marinus. As leader, Romuald decided both spiritual and practical matters. He gave advice on vigils and psalm-saying and devised from his reading of the Fathers what he hoped would become recognised as standard fasting rules for hermits.

For a number of reasons this first community of Romuald's soon broke up. Romuald himself had to leave Cuxa to go to see his father, who had also taken monastic vows, to persuade him to remain faithful to this new vocation. Thereafter Romuald's movements are difficult to follow and there is little to suggest that Damian either knew or was concerned with their exact chronology. The *Life* is largely episodic. Above all it gives an impression of how much Romuald travelled, of how he would gather disciples in any one place, live with them for a time as a hermit, or perhaps build for them a monastery while he lived apart as a recluse and then move on. He was also the friend and advisor of Otto III, whom he wanted to become a monk, and he tried his hand as peace-maker between the insurgents of Tivoli and the imperial camp. He preached to those in orders about the importance of the common life, to clerks and bishops about the heresy of simony, to hermits about the need for obedience to a superior or a rule. Twice, too, he nearly left the eremitical life. In the late 990s he was elected abbot of St Apollinare in Classe, his old house, and under pressure from Otto III he accepted. But because of the strictness of his rule the monks soon regretted their choice and after a few years he resigned. In 1009 he undertook another new venture. He had heard of the martyrdom of Bruno of Querfurt and felt he should emulate it. With papal permission and accompanied by twenty-four disciples he set out for Hungary. As soon as they reached the edges of Pannonia Romuald fell ill. Once he decided to return home he became better, if, on the other hand, he went forward he was again ill. He concluded that it was not God's will that he continue the mission and with about seven of the party he returned to Italy.

This last incident is in many ways typical of Romuald's career. He was an enthusiast, he loved organising and initiating projects, but he often failed to ensure their future or even to carry them through. The fault may not always have been his; it is possible, for example, that he was genuinely reluctant to become abbot of St Apollinare and that it was only after he had taken office that the full difficulties of reconciling his and his monks' views became apparent. It would also be unfair to blame him for the failure, admitted by Damian, of his preaching against simony. It is more remarkable that he tried than that he did not succeed. But Romuald's projects were so often unsuccessful that the cause must sometimes be sought in his own management of affairs. He was clearly a difficult leader – this emerges both from the *Life of Romuald* and from Bruno of Querfurt's *Life of Five Brethren* – jealous, impatient, ever demanding. Above all, his persistent travelling, while it increased the scope of his work, must also have diminished its effectiveness. In Damian's words:

> The holy man burned to do good so that he was never content with what he had done and while at work on some project would soon be rushing off to something different, so that it looked as if he wanted to turn the whole world into a hermitage and for everyone to be joined together in the monastic order.[3]

This restlessness, this fear that whatever he was doing was somehow not sufficiently worthwhile, also explains why it is difficult to know whether Romuald's basic conception of his work ever changed, whether, that is, his plans for Camaldoli differed greatly from his first hermitage of Cuxa. It would seem, in as far as one can tell, that they did not. Damian, writing of Romuald's foundations, suggests that they brought to new places the possibilities of salvation through the eremitical life rather than that they represented developments in Romuald's thought. Moreover, although Camaldoli was to become the head of an order it did not officially do so until the early twelfth century; at the time of its foundation there is no evidence that it was regarded as pre-eminent. Romuald chose to die not there, but at his foundation at Val di Castro.

Romuald's legacy was not, perhaps, a fully fledged eremitical order, but a principle of equal importance to the movement, that is, of obedience in the eremitical life. Both the *Life of Romuald* and the *Life of Five Brethren* stress this. It has already been mentioned how, in the *Life of Romuald* Marinus' disorderly psalm-singing was mocked, and how Romuald devised an eremitical fast based on his readings of the Fathers. Later, when he had returned to Italy, he reprimanded a hermit who was living in the greatest austerity because he had made his own rules and had no spiritual superior. 'If you want to carry the cross of Christ', Romuald told him, 'it is important, above all, not to neglect the obedience of Christ.'[4] One of his own disciples who had broken away from him was to have no prayers said for him on his death in punishment for his disobedience. Most striking of all is the testimony of the *Life of Five Brethren*. Romuald is portrayed there as 'the father of reasonable hermits who live by the law' and in the words of the doge's friend who had known him from Cuxa he was 'the first of our time to live, in great humility, not following his own whims but according to the Conferences of the Fathers'.[5]

Romuald had connections with other monastic reformers. He knew William of St Benigne, he advised the founders of Fonte Avellana, he helped the reform of Farfa. Between him and John Gualbert, founder of Vallombrosa, the other great Italian house of the movement, the links are more tenuous. Gualbert belonged, in fact, to another generation. It was not until 1030 or so that, much against his father's will, he became a monk at the Benedictine house of San Miniato; it is interesting that like Romuald he became a monk only when he was already adult. But there is nothing to suggest that Gualbert was immediately disappointed with the way his house observed the Benedictine Rule. He left only after the simoniacal election of the new abbot. Thereafter he and a companion journeyed, pilgrim style, and they did then stay for a time at Camaldoli. The prior asked them to join but John refused because he

wanted a coenobitic institution and he planned to found his own.
With his companion, therefore, he left Camaldoli and came to
Vallombrosa. There were already two hermits living there who
welcomed their arrival. The story that follows is not, in outline,
unlike that of many other *Lives*: the gathering of disciples, the election of the abbot, the drawing up of customs. What is distinctive
about Vallombrosa is the large part played by John in the religious
revival in Northern Italy. He fought simony, especially in Florence,
with high drama, he reformed a number of monasteries, founded
hospitals, and helped the growth of the canons regular. Moreover,
Vallombrosa was the first house where the new monastic class of
conversi (lay brethren) undoubtedly appear and it was the first house
of the eremitical movement to cling to the strict interpretation of the
Rule of Benedict. For these last two reasons, in particular, it has
sometimes been suggested that there must be a direct link between
Vallombrosa and Cîteaux, but this is no more than a supposition.
Known connections between Italian and French hermits are rare.
Exceptions are the foundation by a monk of Vallombrosa, Andre of
Chézal-Benoît, in Bourges in 1087 and the foundation of Artige by
two Venetians who had come to Limoges on pilgrimage in about
1100. It must also be remembered that Stephen of Grandmont spent
some of his boyhood in Italy and that Bruno of Chartreuse settled
finally at Squillace.

Hermits of the new type appear first in France in about 1030,
possibly in Limoges, in 1028 at Bénévent, certainly in the 1030s in
the following of Herluin of Bec. Bec is, of course, traditionally
associated with the scholastic world, but this was the orientation
Lanfranc gave it. Herluin was a layman who came to the religious
life when he was already nearly forty (even later than Romuald or
Gualbert) and until Lanfranc's arrival the community was marked
by its simplicity and its practice of manual labour. The foundation of
Chaise-Dieu, also to become a Benedictine monastery, may be placed
some ten years after that of Bec. Robert, a canon of Brioude, search-
ed for some time for a more demanding way of life before deciding to
go to the desert, 'for this was what he wanted: to build a monastery,
in solitude, far from the haunts of man, where, in the religious habit,
he could follow the canonical life with two or three companions and
be known to God alone'.[6] In fact, Robert later became archbishop of
Vienne. One of his successors as abbot of Chaise-Dieu, Seguin,
helped the foundation of La Grande Chartreuse.

An early settlement of hermits may perhaps also be found in the Midi, in the secession in 1039 of Rainaud, Odile, Pons and Durand, canons of the cathedral of Avignon, to the ruined church of St Ruf in the suburbs of the city. By 1154, St Ruf was the head of an Augustinian congregation with over a hundred dependent houses. Among others which it influenced were two of eremitical origin; in the 1070s the hermit Gaucher came from Aureil and spent two years at St Ruf so that he could learn its customs; in the early twelfth century it was from there that the hermits of Chaumouzey gained instruction in the Augustinian way of life. But it is a debatable question whether the founders of St Ruf were themselves hermits. The foundation charter of 1039 gives no details of the canons' intentions and until quite recently it was thought that the first custumal was composed only in the twelfth century by the prior Lietbert. A much earlier custumal has, however, now been discovered, one which was certainly used by Lietbert for his own codification and which may have been in use at St Ruf from the very beginning. If this is so then the founders of St Ruf had no new eremitical ideal, but were rather extending the programme of canonical reform initiated by their bishop in the cathedral of Avignon soon after his accession to the see in 1036.

Whatever the traces of the eremitical movement in the first half of the eleventh century there is no doubt that it was only later, in the fifty years between 1075 and 1125, that it reached its height. These years saw the foundation and development of eremitical communities throughout France. They saw the beginnings of Grandmont and La Grande Chartreuse, of Cîteaux, and finally in 1121, of Prémontré. They also saw a great gathering of hermits in the north west, in the forests of Brittany and Maine. From what seems to have been a loose confederation of hermits in this region there came, in the first decades of the twelfth century, the foundations of the hermit-preachers, Bernard of Tiron, Vitalis of Savigny, Robert of Arbrissel, and those less well-known of their disciples: La Flèche, for example, St Sulpice, Etival-en-Charnie. They also had disciples who founded houses further afield; Agudelle (Saintes) was founded by a disciple of Robert of Arbrissel; another follower of his, Geraud de Salles, was responsible for a number of hermitages, including Dalon in the Limousin, Cadouin in Perigord, Grandselve in Toulouse.

Much has been written about those houses of the eremitical movement which were 'successful', that is, which managed to retain their individuality and therefore could continue to offer an alternative to the more traditional forms of the religious life. There is no need to say more of their importance beyond the fact that it was often gained at the expense of smaller eremitical houses which, through diffidence, or lack of resources or skilled leadership, joined them. This was one of the reasons why the ranks of the Cistercians could swell so quickly. Both Pontigny and Morimond, two of the first four daughter houses of Cîteaux, were eremitical in origin. The second daughter house of Clairvaux, too, was founded not by the Cistercians but by a hermit; likewise the fifth, Reigny. The Cistercians also gained through the cession by hermits of houses such as Vauclair (Laon), Bégard (Troyes), Cheminon (Châlons-sur-Marne), Obazine (Limoges), Silvanes (Rodez), Les Dunes (Therouanne). This perhaps may illustrate how widespread the eremitical movement was in France and how, although it was to converge on Cîteaux it was composed in the first instance of independent communities to be found throughout the country. Far from providing the first inspiration for many of the new foundations, Cistercian influence was sometimes felt only in time to refurbish the original ideal. Arrouaise, for example, a community of hermit-canons founded at the end of the eleventh century, was reformed some thirty years later, partly under St Bernard's advice.

In contrast to France, evidence for the eremitical movement in Portugal, Spain and the Empire is slight, though there is some. In Portugal there was at least one house, Alafoes, which was eremitical in origin and which became in time Cistercian. In Spain, a French hermit of the late eleventh century, Pons de Léras, was welcomed in Compostella where he might have stayed but for problems with the language. It is also possible that Romuald had connections with Spanish hermits while he was at Cuxa. As for the Empire, while it is clear that the eremitical movement there did not flourish as it did in France and Italy, its influence was nonetheless felt, especially in Lotharingia. Bruno of Chartreuse and St Norbert, it is true, founded their hermitages elsewhere, but Norbert before he left Germany used to visit a certain hermit Liudolf who, perhaps, was the founder of Lönnig, a priory later dependent on Springiersbach. Springiersbach itself, in Trèves, was the only house of the movement known to have been founded by a woman, a widow. There were also a large number of eremitical foundations in Liège; in Besançon there was a community of hermit-canons (later Cistercians) at Cherlieu; in Cambrai Affligem was founded through the guidance of the archbishop of

Cologne. For Southern Germany it must be remembered that the Hirsau movement with its *conversi* must have given to many laymen the kind of life they could elsewhere have found only within the eremitical movement.

In England, the eremitical movement may be divided into two parts. To the first belong the monks of Evesham: Aldwin, Reinfrid, Aelfwig. These three, in about 1073/4, left their monastery to live in the north the life of poverty of which they had read in Bede. Their story, as we have it from Symeon of Durham, has already been retold by David Knowles and only the outlines need be given here. The monks travelled first to Bede's own house, Jarrow; from there Aldwin went to the brother foundation, Wearmouth, Reinfrid to Whitby (later it was a splinter group from Whitby that founded St Mary's, York). In 1083, monks from both Wearmouth and Jarrow, under Aldwin's leadership, accepted an invitation to go to Durham. Within a space of only ten years the great shrines of early Saxon christianity had been given new life.

Recently, it has been claimed by Derek Baker, that 'though the northern revival has been compared to the eremitical movements which produced Camaldoli, the Chartreuse or Cîteaux' – (this was the view held by Knowles) – 'it stands in fact in sharp contrast to them'.[7] However, the reasons he gives would demolish the eremitical movement *in toto* for there is not a single house that would fit in with his criteria. Firstly, he states 'the northern revival was not the result of random ascetic inspiration but was shaped by custom and tradition'. Certainly, but we have already seen just how historically self-conscious the new hermits were, how carefully they wanted roots and precedents. In their search for the golden age, for the days of true monasticism it was just as natural to use Bede as it was Cassian or the *Lives of the Fathers*. Secondly, according to Baker, 'its sites were not remote, like Cîteaux, inaccessible to men'. We shall see later how the concept of 'remoteness', important as it was, must not be taken too literally. Cistercian houses were nothing like as isolated as was once supposed. Thirdly, 'nor was the life itself strictly eremitical .... They sought to re-establish regular communities, and from the first they accepted recruits and instructed them: Aldwin, as Symeon of Durham records, was "always yearning towards heavenly things, and taking thither such as would follow him".' Which eremitical leader did not?

The second wave of eremitism in England may be found in the first decades of the twelfth century. The earliest communities are perhaps

Nostell (Yorkshire) and Llanthony (Monmouthshire). By 1120, both of these were Augustinian houses, but although it is probable that they date from the first years of the twelfth century the chronology of both is uncertain. In the same way it is difficult to know when there were first hermits at Goathland; there is extant a charter of Henry I's dating from the years 1109–14 granting the hermitage to the priest Osmund and his companions but it would seem likely that this was in fact a restitution, following the displacement of the hermits while the land was afforested.

In 1133 came the foundation of Fountains, by thirteen monks from St Mary's who claimed their life was too lax. Hermits at Kirkstead soon joined them as a daughter house. Other communities of hermits which became Cistercian were those of Radmore, it would seem under pressure from Queen Matilda, and Kirkstall. Finally, it must be remembered that Stephen Harding himself was an Englishman; it was not something he forgot. A letter of his to his former brethren at Sherborne recalls how God had sent him from them so that they might be stimulated to follow his example.

5. Problems of Organisation

The Beginnings of a Community

BEHIND the founding of any hermitage it can be supposed there had been months, in some cases years, of doubts, discussion, speculation. As if to underpin this, the hermits' conversions are rarely represented as sudden, explicable only in the light of miracles, or visions which in a moment transformed the hermits' lives. One such story, that Bruno of Chartreuse went to the desert because he had seen a teacher of Paris rise from his funeral bier with the words 'by the just judgement of God I am condemned' dates in fact only from the fourteenth century. The actual account of Bruno's decision to leave the world he himself gave is the letter to his friend Ralph. It cannot be known how far the conversation he there recalled was the culmination of many others but even after it, as the letter records, Bruno postponed for some time the start of his new life.

There may have been special reasons for Bruno's delay, in particular his role in the case against Manasses, archbishop of Rheims, accused of simony. Other hermits too had commitments which might hold them back. Vitalis of Savigny, for example, had problems escaping from the service of the count of Mortain. Odo of Tournai, master of the cathedral school before his conversion, was allowed to go no further than the outskirts of the city. When he and his companions tried to leave for a more deserted site the citizens of Tournai persuaded the bishop of Noyen-Tournai to order their return. Monks and canons in particular might have difficulty in leaving their communities and there were those who felt forced to escape secretly for fear that if they asked for permission it would be refused. Bernard of Tiron left his abbey in this way at a time when he was afraid the monks wanted to elect him abbot; discovered by them, after three years, he fled further afield to a remote island. Ailbert of Rolduc, who had been prevented once from becoming a hermit by 'friends', probably in this case fellow canons of Tournai, had to content himself for a while with the restoration of a ruined chapel that belonged to the chapter. When he next left the city in search of a hermitage it is very likely that he did so in secret.

This kind of opposition, coupled with the hermits' own uncertainties as to how they should live, helps to explain how very often they would first find a companion with whom they could share both the risks and the excitement of a new life, or a 'soul-friend' who would guide them. St Norbert, for example, after his conversion spent several months with the abbot of Siegburg; for St Anselm, torn between the possibilities of a life of alms-giving, the monastery or the hermitage, the solution was to leave it to Lanfranc, that 'counsellor in a thousand'[1] to decide. Robert of Chaise-Dieu, restless as a canon of Brioude, finally left the community when a certain knight came to him for confession. Here, Robert felt, was a spiritual friend: 'in great joy, he laid bare all the secrets of his heart, bound himself to him and made a pact'.[2] Ailbert, while at work on his chapel, persuaded two of his kin to join him. As many as four of Odo of Tournai's pupils went with him to the ruined sanctuary of St Martin's; six noblemen, moved by the preaching of Wederic of Ghent, set off to become hermits at Affligem. Sometimes, before they settled these small groups would together go on pilgrimage, learning, as had Pons de Léras, 'from religious men everywhere'.[3] Stephen of Obazine on his odyssey first began to look after the needs not only of his own family but also of the poor; next he became a priest; still dissatisfied he discussed with Stephen Mercurius, a disciple of Robert of Chaise-Dieu, whether to leave the world and was urged by him to do so. Then, with a friend, he went to stay with a hermit who lived nearby, who was to teach them both and give them the confidence to start their own community. Sometimes, even at this stage differences of opinion might split up the group. The two companions with whom Bruno of Chartreuse had first left the world never came with him to Grenoble but settled instead at Sèche-Fontaine where they built a priory on land belonging to Molesme. But Bruno collected six other disciples – four clerks and two laymen – and with these he founded Chartreuse.

Where the hermits chose to live is often described in biblical terms – 'a place of horror and infinite solitude' (Deuteronomy xxxii:10). Two things are clear. Such descriptions need not be taken literally, but nor are they to be dismissed. It mattered very much to the hermits that their foundations should as far as possible be built on the margins of society, in the 'waste-lands' which, paradoxically, could be holy and a source of joy, and at the same time the home of devils and a source of terror. But if such houses were to survive, it was clearly vital that the land should be fertile. Many a house had to move to a better site to avoid collapse, often to where there was a river – ('water in the valleys...was rather like petrol today in the desert').[4] There is also no doubt that the hermits sometimes settled on land less wild than the *Lives* suggest. A study of Silvanes, for example ('a place of horror and infinite solitude') has shown no signs that the hermits themselves cleared or drained any new arable land. Peasants had already done it for them. What the hermits at Silvanes did was to manage this newly acquired land with great efficiency and skill. The laybrethren provided an admirable workforce and the hermits showed considerable ingenuity in their use of mills, not only for irrigation and grinding but also for fulling cloth. Even a particularly austere house such as La Grande Chartreuse was not always as isolated as its position suggests. Hugh, bishop of Grenoble, wrote to the laity and clerks of his diocese to tell them that no-one bearing arms was to go through the Carthusian desert, nor was there to be any fishing, bee-stealing or pasturing of animals there.

Often the hermits took whatever land they were given, despite drawbacks, because of the promise of security. Gaucher of Aureil, for example, had been forced to leave his first hermitage in the woods of the Limousin because of monastic claims to the land. When the chapter of Limoges offered him somewhere on their own lands he accepted even though he had in return to give the chapter the right to confirm the prior should the community elect one and he also found that he had to accept churches and their revenues. Subsequently, when Gaucher had trouble with the local clergy this alliance, however costly in other respects, was to prove its worth. Patrons could also in the first months literally keep the hermits going. Archbishop Thurstan of York provided the monks who had left St Mary's with a hermitage at Skeldale and in the early months with food. The citizens of Tournai gave Odo and his companion sufficient resources to enable them to establish themselves in St Martin's. Hermits who had no such backing were forced until they could grow their own crops to rely on foraging – honey and berries if they were lucky – or on the hope – not always justified – of friendly neighbours, and the impression they could make among the faithful by their preaching. They might then, as the *Lives* put it, gain bodily in return for spiritual nourishment. For many hermits the first weeks were clearly precarious. They had, perhaps, only bare essentials. At Affligem, for example, the hermits are described as arriving with 'three loaves they had been given as alms, a cheese and a few tools'.[5]

At Obazine, Stephen and his companion reached their first hermitage on a Friday. On the Sunday they went to a nearby church to say Mass. They were lent shoes for the service, but afterwards nobody asked them to stay for a meal, to their disappointment, for they had had nothing to eat for the last two days. The journey back to Obazine was tiring for it was uphill, but while they were resting on the way they were met by a woman from a neighbouring village who took pity on them and gave them half her loaf and some milk. In later and more prosperous days Stephen used to recall how he had never had any food before or since which tasted as good. But at the time it was only a chance encounter. Once back in their hermitage they had to live for many days on roots and whatever else they could find and it was only when some shepherds had stumbled across them and had spread the news of their existence that they could begin to count on a steady supply of alms from the faithful. Yet this too for a time failed them. A false hermit arrived who also accepted the people's alms, converting what he could not use into money; then, on the night before a promised Mass he disappeared with all his takings. The faithful suspected that Stephen and his companion might act likewise and for a time shunned them.

For immediate shelter and as a centre for their future communities, many hermits chose ruined sanctuaries. This was the kind of place Robert of Chaise-Dieu both wanted and found – 'some little church in a hermitage, ruined and deserted'.[6] But many other hermits must have lived in the open 'with stones for pillows'[7] until they had built themselves huts. These cannot have been elaborate – they might be built only of leaves and branches – nor have taken long to make: even the false hermit from the *Life* of Stephen of Obazine thought it worth his while to make himself one. Before long, however, as their following increased, the hermits were starting on much larger buildings – oratories, houses for the poor, houses for women, and they were also undertaking considerable cultivation of their land.

The Leader

ONCE the hermits had somewhere to live and had gathered together a group of like-minded disciples, they might then, as Robert of Arbrissel's *Life* puts it, begin to establish 'a new family', where there would be 'no discord in their intentions nor in their acts'.[8] It is unnecessarily sceptical to think of such an atmosphere as purely utopian – 'mystic solidarity'[9] is well attested in comparable circumstances – but much would depend within any community on the quality of leadership. It has already been said that the hermits valued obedience, 'the mother of all virtues'[10] and until they had written rules they looked to the authority of their leader; at Obazine, for example, 'since no law of any order had been accepted, the institutes of the master were the rules'.[11]

In most cases there was little question as to who was to lead. The hermit who had originally gathered the following was either assumed or acclaimed as master. There was no formal election and his position was unlikely to be confirmed by either bishop or legate until a later stage in the development of the community, that is, when they had adopted a definite order and customs. But there could be occasions when, for one reason or another, it was not so clear who was to lead. At Obazine, Stephen and his first companion both tried to refuse the role. Their dispute was settled only with outside help – a papal legate intervened and appointed Stephen. There could also be confusion when a group of hermits settled where a hermit was already living. The solution may then have depended on who was a clerk. At Chaumouzey, for example, the hermits put themselves under the priest Anthenor whom they found there leading the solitary life. The chronicle explains:

> Casting aside the things of the world and equally, according to Gospel precept, our own wills, we undertook the fellowship of the common life with him and under him; although we were as yet uncertain which of the holy fathers in the habit of religion we should most closely follow, nonetheless seeking to be under the direction of a single master everyone of us strove, with the help of divine grace to turn away from the broad paths of the old life and to renew the divine image which we have destroyed in the secular world through penitence and to the best of our abilities.[12]

Robert of Arbrissel asked that he should be called neither abbot, nor lord, but rather master. If this suggests that he wanted a more personal and less authoritarian relationship with his disciples than was usual in religious houses it is nonetheless true that in fact eremitical leaders might hold a much more autocratic position than their traditional counterparts. When it came to deciding whether they should become monks or canons then the whole community would be consulted but until then both the making and the enforcing of law was usually in the leader's hands. He would decide when the hermits should work and sleep, what they should eat and wear. Any departure from these regulations had to have his approval. The new hermits, unlike traditional hermits, could not undertake whatever ascetic practices they wanted; thus Christian de l'Aumône had to ask his master for permission to wear something harsher than the linen customary at Gâstines; likewise Gaudentius asked Romuald if it would be all right for him to give up all cooked food. But there is more to the story of Gaudentius than that. Romuald at first gave the permission but was later persuaded by a busybody to rescind it. Gaudentius was so angered that he went to live with a rival of Romuald's who allowed him to follow the regime he wanted. A short time afterwards Gaudentius died. Romuald forbade any prayers for his soul because of his disobedience: only a vision of a tearful Gaudentius softened his heart.

Strictness, the antidote of anarchy, was something the hermits respected and admired. Stephen of Obazine, for example, was praised for being 'strenuous in his discipline and very harsh in the correction of the faults of delinquents'.[13] If anyone raised his eyes in church, smiled even slightly, held his book badly or did anything that could be considered out of order then he was beaten with resounding strokes. A chapter of faults was held daily after either Prime or Mass; corporal punishment was imposed there with an accompanying number of psalms. Stephen's biographer recalled the terror his master's rule had caused yet praised it on the grounds that it was based on the virtues of humility, obedience, poverty, discipline and, above all, charity. At Grandmont it was obedience that was the most important virtue of all. Obedience, according to the *Rule*, was the total offering of oneself to God, even as Christ had offered himself on the Cross. Anyone who wanted to join the community was to look at the Cross and to realise that if he decided to enter he would thereby be giving up all power over his own body, over his eyes, his ears, every limb. Only in this way could his salvation be assured. Whoever, in this world, wilfully refused to obey the commands of a man would find that in the next he would have no choice but to obey all the devils of hell. But the obedient disciple need have no fear. Against him the devil would be powerless.

It would, however, be strange if, at this stage, when rules were still in the making and largely empirical, there were not in any communities arguments and conflicts about the leader's decisions. If these do not appear in many of the *Lives* it may perhaps be because the authors preferred to forget these episodes rather than that they did not take place. It was more edifying to remember occasions when orders were given which, despite their unpopularity, were yet carried out. But not all sources hide the recalcitrance of the hermits against their leaders, or the tensions that might arise within communities. Bernard of Tiron quarrelled with Vitalis of Mortain and, leaving behind buildings which he had worked hard to set up, went off to found his own house. At Arrouaise there was even a fight in which two of the original trio lost their lives. Several attempts were made to murder Romuald and his *Life* is full of resentful, brooding disciples (Gaudentius was only one of many.) A leader's plans might also prove unrealistic. Odo of Tournai, after his unstinting and, in his disciples' eyes, improvident generosity to the poor – he was found to have emptied the house of its supplies – was made to commit the material affairs of his house to 'a prudent man',[14] who was in turn to insist that in future Odo accepted any offerings. Odo had also to promise that he would never again act without consulting the community and that he would give up the attempt to impose on it the ways of the ancients and be satisfied instead with Cluniac customs. Ailbert, the founder of Rolduc, quarrelled with his most influential disciple, Embricon, both on the uses to which to put their resources and on the organisation of their following of women. Ailbert, fearing that his ideals would never prevail, left Rolduc to settle elsewhere. At Aureil, Gaucher's following urged him to teach them the apostolic life. Accordingly, Gaucher went to St Ruf in Avignon to learn the ways of the canons there but when he returned and ordered, among other things, total abstinence from meat, his disciples refused to comply.

What is striking about this criticism is, nonetheless, the limitations. The hermits might oppose their leader but they were not usually capable of acting without him. When Ailbert left Rolduc it was not Embricon or any other of his disciples who took charge, but an outsider, a canon from Rottenbuch who came on the insistence of the archbishop of Salzburg. At Fontaine les Blanches in Tours the hermits, but not their leader, wanted to join some larger house. They pleaded with him, but would not, without his permission, take the initiative themselves.

Whatever his shortcomings it was the vision and personality of the leader which kept together these communities in their early days, which gave them a sense of identity and security when they had as yet no recognisable status. Without a leader of sufficient charisma the community might well disintegrate. So much can be seen by the temporary disbandment of the disciples who had gathered around Bruno at Chartreuse when they learned he was to go to Rome, summoned there by Urban II. It was only Bruno's own call to them to regroup themselves under the leadership of Landuin which led to the continuance of the community. Even if they had already established a rule, hermit-leaders were on their death-beds rightly anxious as to the future of their communities, and might choose someone to succeed them. John Gualbert, when asked how 'the unity of charity and the harmony of peace' was to be kept without him appointed Dom Rudolph to take his place: 'in order that thy charity will always endure among you I charge Dom Rudolph to care for you and to guide you, just as it was my task during my life-time'.[15]

The Laity

THE Benedictine rule presupposes a largely lay community. There could be priests, but their admission was clearly regarded as something exceptional. By the early eleventh century the position was reversed; monasteries were composed almost entirely of clerks. Although laymen could be admitted, in practice this did not often happen and even then the laymen did not seem to have been recognised as the equals of the *nutriti*, those who from childhood had been brought up within the community. But the late eleventh and early twelfth centuries saw a great torrent of lay vocations – 'a huge multitude of men and women rushing to take up the common life'[16] – and at the same time, or so at first sight it seems, the new orders created a place for them: they could become laybrethren (*conversi*). In this role laymen could serve as a point of contact with the world for monks who wanted to keep themselves scrupulously apart from it, they could relieve choir-monks of much of the agricultural work necessary for communities which aimed at self-sufficiency, but they could also by leading a semi-monastic life enjoy a position spiritually superior to that of the ordinary monastic servant. Although these mutual advantages help to explain the success of the institution it is a mistake to see its origin solely in this way; doing so has led to the view that the new monks at a certain stage in their development decided to 'bring in' laymen and confer on them this new status of laybrethren. In certain cases this may be what happened but as a general explanation of the institution it is misleading because it minimises the part played by laymen in the actual formation of the new orders and it gives no indication of what was in fact the case, that many laymen when they became *conversi* lost rather than gained in importance in their community.

Although there were *conversi* in the late eleventh century in the Benedictine house of Hirsau in Southern Germany, they appear mostly in the new eremitical foundations and the first certain reference to them is at Gualbert's foundation of Vallombrosa. There may, however, have been *conversi* very much earlier from the ninth century onwards at Cuxa. This suggestion is of particular interest since Cuxa was the place where Romuald established his first hermitage in the late tenth century. *Conversi* do not appear as such in the *Life of Romuald* but a passage describing the way of life of the servants of his community at Nitria suggests that it was the name rather than the institution which was lacking: '...why talk of the monks, when even the servants of the monks, those who minded the flocks, observed silence and disciplined each other'.[17]

There are some eremitical communities in which, whatever the degree of fraternisation between the two orders, the laymen still seem to have had a separate function from the start. Vallombrosa was one of these. Both monks and laymen are said to have come to John as his disciples and the laymen are described as being 'so faithful in all things that they scarcely differed from the monks'.[18] Yet their activities were different. It was the task of the laymen to go to markets and to attend to all outside business; the clerks, on the other hand, were scarcely allowed beyond the cloister. However, in many other communities there was, in the early years, no such distinction between clerk and lay. It is possible that the numbers were at first too small to make any division seem sensible; in addition, the barrier between those who worked and those who prayed was largely broken down by the eremitical belief in the value of manual labour, the hermit-leaders themselves gloried in doing the most menial tasks. But most important of all is the fact that the eremitical movement attracted so very many laymen and women. In all cases where the sums can be done the laity came always far to outnumber the clergy; at Silvanes, for example, there were in the mid-twelfth century about 20 monks, and 45-50 laymen. Here is Chenu's explanation:

Since the evangelical awakening took place not by a revision of existing institutions but by a return to the gospel that by-passed these institutions, one could predict what its dynamics had to be: witness to the faith, fraternal love, poverty, the beatitudes – all these were to operate more spontaneously and sooner among laymen than among clerics who were bound within an institutional framework.[19]

Some hermitages were founded entirely by laymen. Romuald (although later ordained) was originally a lay-hermit. Six noblemen were the founders of Affligem; three laymen of Flône. Herluin of Bec was a layman, so too was Pons de Léras. Pons, it is true, had among his first companions a priest, but there never seems to have been any doubt at this stage of Pons' leadership. In other houses too, although clerks soon joined, the laymen remained in charge; they were not only the equals of the clerks but even their superiors. Laymen might also form the first community around a hermit-priest so that here too there could be no question of their having a subordinate rank. At Rolduc, for example, Ailbert was a priest but his first disciples were all laymen. It was a matter of note when, five years after the founding of the hermitage, clerks began to join it.

But the influence of the laity in the eremitical movement vanished, as it were, overnight. When the communities became monastic or canonical the laymen, seemingly without question, assumed the status of laybrethren. There was no need for any special ceremony. They remained what they had always been. Something of this can be seen from the description in the *Life* of Stephen of Obazine of the ceremonies when the community became monastic:

Venerable father Stephen was made a monk by a certain abbot who had come with the bishop and immediately was promoted abbot and once he had been consecrated by the bishop he blessed all the clerks of his community as monks, the others he decided were to keep their former status.[20]

Even the lay leaders might become *conversi*. This was the case with Pons de Léras – 'Pons, who always tried to choose the humbler place, stayed as a *conversus*, in the garb of the lay brethren'.[21] A similar situation arose at Flône. When the community there became canonical the three lay founders became *conversi* and there is scant further record of them in the history of the foundation. At Grandmont, where Stephen's closest friend and biographer, Hugh of Lacerta, was a laymen, the *conversi* were given total responsibilities for the administration of the house but nonetheless were clearly regarded as spiritually less capable than the clerks. Moreover, subsequent legislation in some houses (Cîteaux and Arrouaise, for example) specifically forbade any *conversus* from rising to become a monk or canon. In this there is a strange note of submission. The black monk monopoly of monasticism had been destroyed, the clerical, if it went for a time into abeyance, was yet to prove itself – as again in the early history of the Franciscans – very much stronger, even impregnable.

Why was this so? It is possible that both laymen and clerks came to be afraid of the lack of structure of an 'open' hermitage. Always there would be this tension between the Christian ideals of brotherhood and equality and the organisational needs and safeguards of hierarchy. Any lurch in the first direction necessarily provoked reaction, redefinition, a new affirmation of the importance for orthodoxy and stability of *ordo*. Here is St Bernard:

> When men arise from the dead, each in his own order, where do you think this company will be? [i.e. those who have no *ordo*.] If they try to turn to the knights they will throw them out because they have not shared in their trials and dangers. Similarly with the peasants and with the merchants, so that all orders of men in turn will drive them away from their borders because they had not taken part in their work. So what remains to be said – except that people whom every order both rejects and condemns will be put in that place where there is no order but eternal chaos.[22]

Nonetheless, as this passage suggests, there were, in the 'sharpening and redistribution of roles' of the twelfth century, many new parts for the laity. In the words of Gerhoh of Reichersberg:

> Whoever has renounced at baptism the devil even if that person never becomes a cleric...has nonetheless definitely renounced the world; whether rich or poor, noble or serf, merchant or peasant, all who are committed to the Christian faith reject everything inimical to thy name....Every order and absolutely every profession has a rule adapted to its character and under this rule it is possible by striving properly to achieve the crown of glory.[23]

Women

THE eremitical movement attracted a great many women: at the time
of writing Herman of Laon counted those in Norbert's following in
thousands. It is not difficult to find reasons for this. If rank and
status were no hindrance in the beginning of any community, nor
was sex. Women might be converted with their brothers or with their
husbands and their children might come too. Whole families, for
example, were received into the hermitage of St Martin, Tournai.
There were also hermits who took special care of women. Vitalis of
Savigny, for example, was especially concerned with the conversion
of prostitutes, Robert of Arbrissel received at Fontevrault 'widows
and virgins...prostitutes and spurners of men'.[24] In contrast, the
conventional convent of the twelfth century was an exclusive
establishment; the eremitical movement therefore gave to many
women their first chance of leading the religious life. This may be
seen in a letter from bishop Marbod of Rennes to Vitalis of Savigny.
In it Marbod asked Vitalis if he could find a place for a young girl
whose father had become a *conversus* and whose mother could not
afford to buy her entry into a religious house. But noblewomen also
joined the movement. Chroniclers mention this and their testimony is
borne out by the names of some of those concerned: Adela of Mont-
morency was one of Norbert's followers, Petronilla of Chemille of
Robert of Arbrissel.

There were, however, special problems for women who wanted to
be hermits. It was clearly difficult for them to start a foundation.
They needed men to protect them, to build and do other heavy work
for them (although they did a great deal of manual work themselves)
and for the administration of the sacraments. They had therefore to
find some group of men who were willing – and not all of them were
– to accept the responsibility of their joining them. The problem
then arose as to how close the association was to be. In some cases it
might be possible to establish the women in an entirely separate
foundation. But when women joined a hermitage early in its development it was more natural and in some ways easier for them to form a
double community, generally with the women under the jurisdiction
of the abbot. At Robert of Arbrissel's foundation of Fontevrault,
however, it was the women who were in charge – as had been the case
with many early medieval double monasteries. In time, the women of

these double communities came to be strictly cloistered but while the
communities were still in the making the mixing of the sexes could
cause tension from within and criticism from without. Robert of Arbrissel's conduct was extreme – he is said to have slept among his
women disciples, perhaps as the ultimate test of victory over his body
– but in other communities there were less dramatic solutions to be
worked out.

Gaucher of Aureil, for example, since he knew that 'neither sex
was excluded from the kingdom of heaven',[25] welcomed both men
and women disciples, and built for the women a house very near his
own cell: 'He sought to build the heavenly Jerusalem with walls of
both sexes and therefore built a convent of the sisters a stone's throw
from his own cell, sharing his poverty with men and women alike'.[26]
The arrangement is alleged to have troubled Stephen of Grandmont,
said at that time to be a disciple of Gaucher's. He told Gaucher he
was afraid the company of women might endanger his soul and he
therefore asked if he could live at a little distance from Gaucher's
cell. Later he moved further away, and this, according to the *Life* of
Gaucher, was the beginning of Grandmont. Much of this story must
be regarded as apocryphal; there is no reason to suppose that
Stephen of Grandmont ever was, in fact, a disciple of Gaucher's; but
there certainly were a great number of women at Aureil and the problem of their presence could have been real. So it was at Rolduc.
When Embricon joined Rolduc his wife came too and she in turn was
soon joined by other women. But the original buildings had not been
designed for this development. Men and women had to share the
same crypt for the Offices and this, to the founder Ailbert, seemed
wrong. He tried to move the women to a different site but led by Embricon's wife, and backed by Embricon himself, they refused to go.
Ailbert, because of this and other disagreements with Embricon, left
to found another hermitage. But the question of where the women
should live and of the administration of their house was to trouble
Rolduc intermittently for another thirty years. Women were finally
only allowed to belong to the community at all because they were
needed for the mending and – a characteristic eremitical argument
– because women had administered to the apostles. At Obazine,
where they were said to number more than 500, the women were
moved from their first site, since it was too near the men's buildings,
to a place further afield. Elaborate precautions were still taken to

prevent contacts. The sacrament was passed through a little window and food was distributed through a system of double doors. The women worked hard at household duties, the grimier (apparently) the better and they could also bring up their own children, in the case of boys until they were five-years-old when the monks took over their care. (The presence of these children suggests either the conversion of whole families or of prostitutes or victims of rape.) One such child, on being asked by the monk who had come to fetch him about the women who had been looking after him, showed that he did not know the word; as far as he was concerned it was sisters not women who had brought him up. But, yes, he told the monk, he would like to see what women were. The monk pointed to some nearby goats and said 'those are women'. The joke was much enjoyed when the child was later heard boasting that he had seen some women grazing by those 'who had a more exact, but not a happier knowledge of women'.[27]

The immense difference in character between a monastery of oblates and a community that had grown up to fulfil the spiritual needs of adult men and women has been emphasised by Jean Leclercq. He believes 'it is possible to show that the deep and spontaneous attitude to femininity and women was much more positive in Bernard and in members of the new orders than it had been...love for God is often and preferentially symbolised by love between a man and a woman'.[28] All the same, as the anecdote from Obazine shows, there was hardly a natural acceptance of women. The fundamental tension remained: woman was Eve as well as the Virgin, Delilah as well as Mary Magdalene. The paradox could not be resolved and it was easier, in practice, not to try. In the twelfth and thirteenth centuries, therefore, both the Cistercians and the Premonstratensians did their best (however unsuccessfully) to disown or ignore their women followers. Devotion to women saints, on the other hand, and to the Virgin in particular, was encouraged. Christ himself was seen not only as a bridegroom but also as a mother. The intense revival of such feminine religious imagery, especially in Cistercian communities, has recently been examined by Caroline Walker Bynum. She suggests that it expresses not only new concepts about Christ but also about the nature of leadership but that it does not necessarily reveal anything about 'actual women'.[29] The very many who in the thirteenth century felt the need to become beguines tell, perhaps, the fuller story.

6. Observances

The Poor Men of Christ

'THE poor men of Christ': this, first and foremost, was how the hermits saw themselves. Their love of poverty might be expressed as a wish to imitate Christ's own poverty; Stephen of Obazine, for example, at the start of his pilgrimage, abandoned all earthly concerns 'so that poor and naked himself he might follow the poor Christ'.[1] It might also be seen as a response to Christ's teaching on poverty. Christ's advice to the rich man (Matthew xix:21), his warnings on the difficulty for the wealthy in entering the kingdom of heaven, these were the texts frequently quoted to explain and justify the hermits' conversions. Even if the hermits, as laymen, had not actually read the passages, this did not make them any the less relevant. Here is the foundation charter granted by Henry of Verdun, describing the beginnings of Flône:

> He who does not renounce all that he possesses cannot come to me, said the Lord. Having understood rather than read this truth, three faithful laymen, ...having given up all worldly desires, chose to live in a solitary house in that place which is called Flône.[2]

Poverty was, of course, also an essential part of the Benedictine way of life. It is all the more striking therefore that it was not only laymen and secular priests who became hermits for the sake of poverty, but even black monks themselves. Richard of St Mary's, York, for example, planned to leave his house and to establish a hermitage 'so that he could follow the poor Christ in voluntary poverty'.[3] The black monk concept of poverty was thus clearly regarded by those who wanted to become hermits as inadequate. Nor is it difficult to see why. For it was concerned only with personal poverty, whereas the hermits were interested also in communal poverty, and the 'powerlessness' which this entailed. To the black monks of the eleventh century the material prosperity of a monastery was a sign of its general well-being; reform meant not only the enforcement of discipline but also the restoration of revenues; God was to be glorified not only through the individual piety of the monks but also by the magnificence of the monastic buildings. To the hermits, on the other hand, the community had no more right to riches than had the monk. It was wrong, they felt, that anyone who had taken a vow of poverty should be able to enjoy in his house a splendour he could never have attained in the world. Communal wealth was, moreover, contrary to the doctrine that a Christian, and particularly a monk, should be dead to the world and free from its preoccupations: 'No man that warreth entangleth himself with the affairs of this life; that he may please him who has chosen him to be a soldier' (II Timothy xi:4). Too many possessions were seen as a direct contravention of this text. They encouraged greed and acquisitiveness, they led to quarrels and law-suits and they made it impossible for the monk to fulfil his true vocation of service to God. Litigious monks were one of the chief targets of the new hermits. Rainaud, in his letter to Ivo of Chartres, upbraided them with Christ's words: 'if any man will sue thee at law and take away thy coat, let him take away thy cloke also' (Matthew v:40);[4] St Norbert gave as one of the conditions on which he would agree to be abbot of St Martin the cessation of all lawsuits; the reformers of St Mary's argued in praise of the Cistercians that they alone 'possessed nothing' and were not covetous.[5]

The difference between the eremitical and the black monk concept of poverty may be seen in the first instance in the disposal of the novices' goods. The hermit might give away any possessions he had to the poor before he left the world. St Norbert, for example, after the Council of Fritzlar had passed sentence on him for preaching without a licence, resigned his ecclesiastical benefices before the archbishop of Cologne, sold his patrimony and gave the money to the poor. For himself he kept only his priestly vestments and some ten marks of silver and this money too when he reached Huy he gave away. Black monks, by contrast, had to give their possessions to the community they were entering and indeed they thereby bought their place. To join an eremitical community such an endowment – although sometimes welcomed – was nonetheless unnecessary; it was said of John Gualbert 'he preferred to receive a poor man of genuine austerity rather than a rich man with all his property'.[6] The hermits might impose tests of humility – Odo of Tournai, for example, made one convert move a huge stone beyond the city of Tournai – but they were not interested in property qualifications. They might, as Odo did, give any money they received to the poor, or they might even refuse to accept anything that novices had to offer. This was so in the first years at Affligem and also at Grandmont under Stephen – 'he would have thought it simony if anyone had entered religion promising earthly possessions of any kind'.[7]

The hermits might also refuse to hold certain kinds and amounts of property and in this way too, they broke away from traditional monastic practice. If a monk was dead to the world, then, the hermits argued, he should not hold mills or manors; nor, unless he exercised a care of souls, had he any right to tithes and churches. Such views are to be found in their most extreme form at Grandmont. The hermits there refused these (and other) categories of property; moreover, they would not even give themselves the legal right to the land on which they were established, that is they refused to hold any charters which would have guaranteed their ownership: 'in any other monastery you can find herds and acres of land....here, only the Cross and poverty'.[8] Patristic texts as well as evangelical teaching were used to explain these prohibitions. The Cistercians, for example, based their refusal to hold mills, manors, churches, altars, ovens and burial grounds in the light of the Benedictine rule, saying that:

> when St. Benedict said that a monk should make himself a stranger to the activities of the world he bore clear witness to the fact that these things should no longer have any place in the activities or hearts of monks who ought to conform to the etymological origin of their name by fleeing from them.

Tithes too, they refused as a 'right usurped from others' since 'the holy fathers have never taught that monks should have them'.[9] Others who saw their renunciation of ecclesiastical revenues as a return to the ways of the early church were the hermits of Tournai. Odo, according to the chronicler of his house, Herman, 'said that such revenues should be owned only by clerics, not by monks. And his determination in this respect conformed to the life and practices of the monks of old'.[10]

Not all eremitical communities, however, had such property scruples. Some were ready to accept whatever they were offered – the gift of the allod of Chaumouzey, for example, included serfs, a church and various ecclesiastical oblations. Other communities refused ecclesiastical but not feudal sources of revenue: to veto both, as did Cîteaux and Grandmont, was the exception rather than the rule, and Cîteaux herself was prepared to allow the affiliation of

Savigny in 1147 although this was a congregation which possessed tithes. It would, however, be a mistake to measure the strictness of any hermit's concept of poverty in terms of the number of different kinds of property he refused. The *Life of John Gualbert,* for example, mentions only that John would not accept churches, but the miracles attributed to him show how uncompromising he was felt to be on the more general subject of monastic wealth. He had, for instance, heard of an abbot who had accepted the whole of a novice's patrimony and he therefore went to him and asked to see the charter of donation. Having inspected it he tore it up and called for the house to be afflicted by divine punishment. Shortly after he had left the house was indeed burnt and John refused even a glance back at it. Another story, recently analysed by R. I. Moore, sheds further light on Gualbert's sensitivity about property, how he came to feel it was wrong to commandeer cattle from a nearby flock even when his intentions – to distribute the carcasses to the poor – were honourable. 'Arbitrary exactions' of any kind were seen to be incompatible with true poverty.[11] The miracles attributed to Stephen of Obazine show a similar concern. A pair of oxen belonging to a certain peasant were rescued by Stephen from the hands of a knight who was seizing all he could to pay off gambling debts; one of the local count's officials, who insisted on taking the meagre provisions of a widow, and a few hens, as dues and who kicked her when she protested, was struck dead on his subsequent journey, with no time even to receive the viaticum.

The hermits thus hated money, wealth and its power with an intensity more usually associated with the Franciscan movement. Gifts of any kind troubled them deeply – it was the refusal of a silver vase by two hermits of Fonte Avellana which first attracted Damian to their order. Money itself was repugnant. Once, on a journey, a certain hermit offered a companion of Bernard of Tiron 18 coins 'that would at least provide them with something for the first few days of their journey. When the man of God learnt that money was being carried with them he was not a little incensed. "Either you cease to be my companion", he said, "or you cease carrying these coins"'.[12]

The monetary explosion of the eleventh and twelfth centuries brought with it revived possibilities for that old vice, avarice. Lester K. Little has shown how preoccupied the twelfth century was with this sin. According to Gerhoh of Reichersberg (1093–1169) in *On the Fourth Nightwatch* avarice was the 'unfavourable wind' of their time, the fourth period of Christian history. To counter each 'unfavourable wind' (the other three were the persecutions, the heresies and the corruption of morals), God sent help. Those chosen to fight avarice were disciples who had renounced all their possessions, in short the 'poor men of Christ'.[13]

Manual Labour

WORK, of a manual kind, was the way in which hermits, traditionally, were expected to avoid the problem and spiritual dangers of idleness. Among the new hermits and especially among those who had rejected any of the customary sources of monastic revenue it was a matter both of principle and of necessity. Many of the new communities had every intention of supporting themselves entirely by the work of their own hands. The only help they considered it legitimate to accept was that given in alms. Odo of Tournai, for example, who was supported in his first year by offerings from the citizens of Tournai, hoped his community would live 'solely from the labour of their hands, from the land cultivated by their teams and from the nourishment of their herds'.[14] At Affligem where, as at Tournai, ecclesiastical revenues were refused the hermits tried by their own work to produce enough both for themselves and for a tenth of their revenue to be given to the poor:

> When the principle of our way of life had been confirmed and the path of the regular life entered upon we could not discover a more rightful or devout path of salvation than that we should gain nourishment and clothing by the labours of our hands and remain content with these.[15]

For the new hermits work had clearly a special, regenerative character: Rupert of Deutz was later to mock those monks 'who place almost all their hope in manual labour'.[16] To value it was to reject both the economic boom of the twelfth century and all secular distinctions. Clerk and layman, noble and peasant, all could do their share and indeed must if the apostolic life was to be a reality. Had not St Paul in his letters to the Thessalonians described how he had worked, when he was with them, to avoid being an expense? – 'not that we were obliged to do this, but as a model for your own behaviour' (II Thess iii:9-10). Among the new hermits Ailbert of Rolduc took up this text. He worked, according to the *Annales*

Rodenses, 'as blessed Paul is said to have done'.[17] But St Paul was not the only authority used. The Fathers too had practised and recommended manual labour. At Springiersbach, in the diocese of Trier, the hermits mentioned particularly the precepts of Augustine and Benedict:

> It would not seem to be unworthy or useless to commemorate two fathers, St. Augustine and St. Benedict, who ascribed perfection to no religion without manual labour, so much so that both of them not only prescribed it but also conserved the statutes of earlier people and both of them left it in writing at what time those who embraced the imitation of the apostolic life on earth must labour so that they should merit in heaven the glorification of their beatitude.[18]

Such an interpretation of Benedict's rule was, for the eleventh and twelfth centuries, revolutionary; it was to become one of the central points in the debate between Cluniacs and Cistercians. It is not certain that Benedict himself had ever intended his monks to do much agricultural work but even the hours set aside in his *Rule* for some kind of manual occupation had come by then to be regarded as largely optional, as a way of keeping busy but of no particular merit if something else could be found to fill the time. The chapter on work in the *Rule* – Chapter 48 – made possible both this and the hermits' opposing view. It begins: 'Idleness is the enemy of the soul. The brethren therefore must be occupied at stated hours in manual labour and again at other hours in sacred reading'. To the hermits this meant that work was an imperative, to the black monks what was important was not Benedict's solution but the problem, if idleness could be prevented in some other way then the actual number of hours given to work could be shortened. There is ambiguity too, at the end of the chapter, on the problem of work on the land: '...if the circumstances of the place or their poverty require them to gather the harvest themselves let them not be discontented; for then are they truly monks when they live by the labour of their hands, like our fathers and the apostles'. By the eleventh and twelfth centuries emphasis had long been placed on Benedict's 'if': to assert, as did the hermits, that what was important was 'for then are they truly monks', was to challenge both the accepted theory and the practice of the religious life.

In the first years of any community there was plenty of work at hand in the actual building of the hermitage and its church and in the cultivation of land. Although sometimes, as at Silvanes, land had already been cleared this was not always the case. Hermits might be given as much land as they could bring under cultivation. The work might be very heavy and if it was especially menial, so much the better. Postulants at Grandmont had to be asked whether they could dig ditches, carry wood and manure. Whereas at Cluny the liturgy had become so lengthy that there was hardly any time for work, for the hermits the problem was reversed: it was fitting in the liturgy that was difficult. Bernard of Tiron had to shorten the psalmody to make more hours available for work. At Obazine the hermits worked night and day, at day on the buildings, collecting stone, cutting down trees, at night by candlelight making whatever the community might need. Anyone who was physically too weak to join in the hard daytime labouring was allowed a less taxing task, such as the copying of books. Hired workers were also used but the hermits took great pride in developing skills themselves. Bernard of Tiron who had himself, when he first became a hermit, asked to be taught ironwork later gathered around him vine-dressers, goldsmiths, stonemasons and carpenters in the hope that each would practise his own craft.

Manual work for the hermits was not simply penitential but rather a means of recreating the primitive simplicity and equality of the Garden of Eden. 'Are we not', wrote Ailred of Rievaulx, 'beholding nobility turning its back on the world in answer to the call of conversion, casting aside swords and spears in order to join with us as we earn our bread with the work of our hands, just as though they were true serfs.'[19] This may well be an idealised picture but it is worth noting that in the earliest Cistercian manuscripts, dating from the time of Stephen Harding, monk and laybrother are in fact depicted at work together, both chopping down the same extrememly realistic tree. Moreover, according to Le Goff, 'there is abundant evidence from every quarter that the spiritual attitude towards labour was undergoing a crucial development through practice'.[20] and that in these circumstances the old division of society into those who worked, those who prayed and those who fought 'receded before more elaborate categorizations, which took hold thanks to a growing awareness and sanctioning of the diversification and division of labour'.[21]

It is a great disappointment that we do not have the promised discussion of *The Orders and Callings of the Church* on manual labour: the manuscript may have been lost, but it is also possible that

the work was never completed. Nonetheless, the author of this tract
(a canon, probably of Liège of the early twelfth century) does discuss
at some length a number of the problems caused by the practice of
manual labour.[22] He is writing about hermit-canons, that is, those
canons who, in his description, have chosen to live far from men.
First, he praises the way of life of such canons – 'I praise the
magnanimity of this way of life; ....I love their great humility': then
comes the criticism, 'I declare there is a measure to be held to in
everything'. What is troubling the writer is that 'priests and even an
abbot in this order of canons' are 'milking their own ewes and clean-
ing stables'. 'I can hardly believe it', he exclaims. On the one hand
such humility is astonishing and admirable, on the other it is deeply
upsetting to the writer's notions of ritual purity that as a result of
such work these priests may be administering the sacrament with
filthy clothes. Surely they could 'clean the church floor, not the
stable of horses'. Or they could dig, cut wood, reap, plant, sew – all
these are tasks which could be carried out 'with reverence for the
body of the Lord'. These concerns, interesting in themselves, must
also dispel any reservations about the reality of the hermits' work-
forces, any suspicions that they are literary exaggerations.

Finally, M. Duby has recently suggested how vital is the role of
manual labour in the development of the new values of the twelfth
century, the 'awareness of progress', 'the spectacle of a world
transformed by man's efforts'. 'Here, with the labours of the settlers
ceaselessly clearing new land was born the idea that civilisation grows
like a plant...that each generation takes up the task from the hands
of its predecessors and must carry it further toward its goal'.[23]

Hospitality and Alms-giving

CARE of the poor and the sick as a way of serving Christ has its clearest
justification in Matthew xxv, in the description of the last judgement
and the reward to the just because of their good works: 'whereupon
the just will answer, Lord, when was it that we saw you hungry and
fed thee or thirsty and gave thee drink, or naked and clothed thee?
and the king will answer, believe me, when you did it to the least of
my brethren you did it unto me.' This text was re-echoed in many
Lives. Of Pons de Léras, for example, it was written 'it was his

custom and held by him as an unwritten law to receive everyone into the guest house, to help those in need, to revive the poor, to clothe the naked, to bury the dead'.[24] There was also, according to *The Orders and Callings of the Church* an Old Testament model. Hermit-canons there 'take pains to provide such hospitality and kindness for guests that they are rightly said to be similar to Abraham and Lot who used to receive angels since they loved guests'.[25]

Some poor relief and the receiving of guests had always been part of the Benedictine way of life – Benedict, also basing his attitude on Matthew xxv, had ordered that all guests were to be treated with honour and alike, but in fact a two-tier system had developed with a guesthouse for those who came on horse and an almshouse for foot pilgrims. The monks, if they feasted the first did not altogether forget their responsibilities to the second class of visitors but all the same they showed little awareness of the actual misery of poverty. The poor, after all, would always be with them – all that could be done, all that was needed was a gesture. Charity became ritualised: gifts were given to certain poor men at particular times. Almsgiving became a part of the liturgy.

The hermits, as the poor men of Christ, had a different perspective. Care of the poor and the sick was at the heart of true religion. Poverty was an honourable estate. 'It is your privilege', wrote Stephen of Grandmont, 'to talk to the poor',[26] and as if to make it quite clear to the hermits of Grandmont that they themselves belonged to this class Stephen allowed his community to accept a poor man's alms. The 'liberality' of bishops and abbots towards the poor must be compared (according to M. Sigal) with this sharing, by the hermits, of the experiences of poverty, the literal embrace of the sick and the deformed. Abelard's view – that a monastery if it does not give away all its surplus is guilty of the deaths of those it could have supported – is no more than a development of earlier eremitical thought. Ailbert of Rolduc's biographer, for example, reports him as saying that he would help the poor whose immortal souls were made in the image of God rather than spend money on buildings that were bound to perish. Odo of Tournai refused to have gold crosses for similar reasons – 'he did not desire to make gold crosses but to give away all the money that was brought to him by the poor and needy'.[27] Both Robert of Chaise-Dieu and Richard of Fountains are described as giving away all their food to poor men who chanced to ask for it; Stephen of Obazine ordered all livestock (except the oxen) to be killed as food for the poor when there was no longer any grain; John Gualbert sold the pluvials of the church of Vallombrosa to raise money for the poor.

Examples could be multiplied but it is time to look more closely at those houses the hermits founded where there were special buildings for the sick, lepers for example, at Fontevrault, or for travellers. These last are generally called hospitals – bearing in mind that 'the modern use of the word may mislead us....a hospital catered at the preference of its founder for the sick, the aged, destitute or travellers and frequently for all at the same time. It was a refuge or group home rather than a medical establishment.[28] 'Hospice' would perhaps be a better translation. At Prémontré, there was a hospice for men and women. At Mass, according to Norbert, the brethren could show their love of God, in confession, their care for themselves, but the hospice alone gave them the opportunity to put into practice their love of their neighbour. Two other well-documented examples of hermit-hospices are Affligem in Cambrai and Flône, though in both cases the idea seems to have come not so much from the hermits themselves as from the bishops whom they consulted about which way of life to adopt and who thereupon advised them to establish hospices on sites known to be dangerous to travellers. The choice of Affligem had particular significance since it was the hermits themselves who had formerly terrorised it as robbers.

Flône and Affligem – and many other hospices – were lay foundations but they were soon joined and controlled by clerks who do not seem to have shared the first hermits' enthusiasm for hospice work. There could be no doubt that charity, on whatever scale, might over-tax the resources of a house, especially if it was trying at the same time not to amass property and to be self-sufficient, and that the continual search for food for the poor, and for the community, was wearing and time-consuming. Stephen of Obazine's biographer has left a description of how the saint, in times of famine, would frantically search all the surrounding granaries for secret reserves, how he would buy up grain on credit and then not be able to pay, how the brethren would spend nearly all day distributing food to the poor, preparing two or three batches of dough which they then took away to cook. It is therefore perhaps not surprising to find a document for Flône, some thirty years after its foundation, in which a distinction is made for financial reasons between the church and the hospice and which makes it clear that the one is the concern of the clerks, the other of the laity. The first procurator of the hospital was Folcuin, one of the original founders of Flône. Whether as lay brethren or hospice workers, the laity were once again confined to Martha's sphere.

Liturgy and Private Devotions

TRADITIONALLY, the psalter was the basis of the hermit's prayer life and it is clear that those hermits who, as laymen, did not know it set about to learn it. Romuald, it will be remembered, thought his early singing of it both funny and unprofessional. Other groups of lay-hermits may have had similar difficulties. We must accept that in any community the development of its own forms of worship was a slow process – often a gradual blending of local practices – and that in most cases it cannot be uncovered. There has, however, been much research on the evolution of the Cistercian liturgy.

The first Cistercians followed the traditional Cluniac services. They had taken with them a breviary and a psalter from Molesme and they were allowed to copy the breviary before returning it. While doing so they are said to have noticed mistakes in the manuscript and they therefore decided to revise it. Work subsequently began on the Bible, the Ambrosian hymns and plainchant with the intention of finding the most authentic form of each. The results were not entirely satisfactory and therefore further liturgical changes were made in the time of St Bernard, much to the confusion of Obazine. When the hermit-monks there became Cistercian they had to alter their liturgical books 'which they had recently, with a great deal of work, made according to the monastic order to Cistercian usage'.[29] They were amazed and rather taken aback at the difference since their first books had come to them from Dalon which in turn had taken them from Cîteaux – but before the days of St Bernard.

The principle behind the Cistercian changes was, and was clearly stated to be, the same as inspired their other reforms, namely the wish to restore primitive monastic practices, in particular as found in the Benedictine *Rule*. They therefore omitted many of the customary offices, prayers, hymns, commemorations and processions. This shorter liturgy made possible the return to the periods of manual labour which the *Rule* prescribed, and which were not only desirable in themselves but also, as other hermits found, very necessary. In the early years at Tiron, as we have mentioned, Bernard's followers found they had no time for all the work needed for clearing and cultivating their hermitage and they therefore implored Bernard to shorten the psalmody. Bernard was wary of the change, and according to his *Life* it was only after a vision had assured him that he could with impunity depart from the traditions of the church that he gave his consent. Another way of shortening liturgical obligations was to say Mass less often. It was at this time customary in black monk houses for there to be two celebrations each day but this was not usual in eremitical houses. At Chartreuse, for example, there was a conventual celebration only on Sundays and feast days.

Robert of Arbrissel, when he knew that he was dying, asked to be buried among the sick and the lepers of Fontevrault and not at Cluny 'where they have grand processions'.[30] If this suggests that the hermits favoured liturgical austerity it is nonetheless not the whole picture. At Obazine, for example, Saturdays were celebrated with two Masses in honour of the Virgin and the hermits, it is said, worked only that they should not seem like the Jews. On Sundays there was a procession throughout the cloister and other feast days were kept with singing of the kind associated with great monasteries – 'for indeed it was a great monastery, …rich in virtue if not in domain'.[31] The hermits may indeed have given work a sacral character, and because of it had to shorten their liturgy but in no way did they undervalue it. Geoffrey of Chalard's dying words to his followers were that they must not neglect the divine office.

Particular Offices might be used by the hermits for their private as well as their communal devotions. Stephen of Grandmont, for example, is said to have been especially fond of the Office of the Trinity and to have said it night and day all the time he was at Muret. But the most common form of private devotions remains singing of the psalter, and genuflexions. Romuald assured his disciples that it was better to sing one psalm 'from the heart' than to run through a hundred unthinkingly[32] but all the same psalm-singing seems to have remained primarily an ascetic feat. Damian gave as examples to be praised hermits who said two, three or even four psalters a day. Both psalm-singing and genuflexions might be done during some other occupation, while working, for example, or in the case of psalm-singing, while on a journey. Gaucher of Aureil had the psalter always on his lips, except when eating or sleeping. Stephen of Grandmont is said to have prostrated himself so frequently that his hands and knees became thick and hard like a camel's (a classic description) and his nose misshapen.

Other ascetic practices attributed to hermits include the wearing of hair or chain shirts, cold baths, flagellation. Descriptions of these are never lacking, but they make it all the more difficult to uncover the individual act of piety from the conventions of the hagiographer. The crowning glory of personal prayers was clearly the 'gift of tears', tears which came not 'drop by drop, but like a stream'[33] but even this still leaves us in the dark about the nature of the prayers. There is extant a collection of prayers attributed to John Gualbert, but in the judgement of Dom Wilmart there is no reason to think that it was in fact composed by him nor, according to Wilmart, does it differ in kind from the manuals possessed by the black monk houses of the twelfth century.

The hermits' devotion to Mary Magdalen, however – they frequently dedicated their churches to her – does suggest new trends and preoccupations, a concern, above all, with penance and contrition. A charter from Adalbero, bishop of Liège, for example, recording the foundation of Castert, states how a certain Bovo came to him to ask for land where he could build an oratory so that he might for his sins follow the example of 'the holy penitent' Mary Magdalen. This stress on private sins and their expiation (as opposed to the notion of corporate prayer to help the sins of the world) does in itself point the way to the spirituality of the mid-twelfth century, to the greater introspection characteristic of the writings of Guy of Chartreuse and of St Bernard. Something of this may be found too for the first generation of hermits in the *Liber Sententiarum* of Stephen of Grandmont: how a man prays, in what position, does not matter. What is important is the love which he brings to his prayers, the awareness of his own nature, the recognition of himself as a sinner.

So much has been written of the new spirituality of the twelfth century that it is tempting to grind the sources 'in a mortar' as Peter Damian recommended for the Psalms[34] in the hope that it can be shown without a shadow of doubt how the roots of these developments are eremitical. But it is on the whole the traditional framework, whatever the modifications, that is most clearly expressed. However, there are exceptions such as the *Liber Sententiarum* and, above all, the illustrated manuscripts made at Cîteaux in the first quarter of the twelfth century. Here, for the first time in the West for many centuries is Christ at the breast; the picture in the words of Richard Southern is 'a compendium of the new devotion to the humanity of the Saviour and his earthly mother'.[35] It is also a striking illustration of the vigour and originality of Cîteaux before St Bernard became dominant.

Food and Clothing

THE adage 'you are what you eat' can, of course, be reversed. A refusal to eat meat for example may be, as one monastic historian has described it, a 'socio-economic protest',[36] a statement of allegiance and priorities. For this one need go no further than Genesis xxv:27-29: 'Esau was a cunning hunter; a man of the field; and Jacob was a plain man dwelling in tents. And Isaac loved Esau because he did eat of his venison, but Rebekah loved Jacob. And Jacob sod pottage...'

The significance that could be attached, in the twelfth century, to details of food and clothing reached hyperbolic proportions in the clashes between St Bernard and Peter the Venerable. For the earlier period we have the debate recorded by Ordericus Vitalis,[37] said to have been held at Molesme between Robert, as abbot, and his community. Robert asks his monks to keep strictly to the *Rule of Benedict* and not to wear 'breeches and shirts and lambskins'. His monks are outraged, breeches are 'useful and modest', St Benedict expected clothing to be chosen according to local custom and in the same way so should food. Of course those who have olive oil do not need to use lard, but this can only reasonably be applied to the monks of Italy and Palestine.

This discussion is unusual for several reasons, not least because it is about a schism within a community. The outcome is well-known. Robert and the twelve monks who agree with him leave to found Cîteaux. Pope Urban intervenes, returns Robert to Molesme as abbot but gives everyone the right 'to make an initial choice of the way of life desired', on condition that he would be 'indissolubly bound to abide by it all his life'. Few other communities had such clear-cut points of departure and their customs emerged more slowly. For example, to some extent, especially in their early days, the hermits ate what they could, what they were given in alms or whatever they found in their hermitages. The latter might yield little beyond roots or herbs but there might also be chance finds such as the honeycomb when Bernard of Tiron first arrived in the forest of Craon and it is likely that nuts were plentiful there. The hermits' staple diet remained, however, purposefully meagre. It was composed largely of cereals and vegetables. In the *Life of Romuald*, for example, the basic foods mentioned are beans and boiled chickweed; at Muret, from the day he became a hermit, Stephen lived on bread and water, though he occasionally had too a small and rather tasteless drink made of wheat. Fish were miraculously caught from normally barren waters in honour of Romuald when he arrived once at Sitria and for John Gualbert when he was feeling ill on a journey back to Vallombrosa after visiting other foundations. Foods that were often forbidden were fat, meat and wine but there is considerable difference in the extent to which the hermits were prepared to carry out these prohibitions. John Gualbert thought meat could be eaten if nothing else was available. Stephen of Obazine, on the other hand, would not even let men he was employing on a new building eat it. If they could not do the work of God without meat, then he would rather they left.

There is the question not only what, but also when the hermits ate, and of what they meant by fasting. At least two definitions were possible. In Peter Damian's rule for Fônte Avellana to fast was to eat only bread, salt and water. In the *Constitutions of Camaldoli*, however, this was abstinence – fasting meant only one meal a day. This also seems to have been how the word was used at Obazine. The hermits there are described as fasting throughout the week but it is also clear that they had a meal every evening with cooked vegetables. The evidence of the *Life of Romuald* is more difficult to unravel. Romuald is said to have devised a rule of fasting which he hoped would come to be observed by all hermits. He had at first, under the influence of the *Lives of the Fathers*, fasted from Monday to Friday, but on reading the *Life of St. Sylvester* he changed this and fasted on Saturday instead of Thursday, and it was this which he prescribed as the eremitical fast. On Thursdays and Sundays the hermits had a kind of fish soup and vegetables. It might seem at first as if fasting here meant, as in Damian's other writings, a diet of bread, water and salt. But it is difficult to reconcile this interpretation with a passage in the *Life of Romuald* where the hermit Gaudentius asked his master if he could renounce all 'dishes' and live only on bread, water, apples and raw vegetables. Romuald, as we know, granted him permission but then rescinded it on the advice of another hermit who claimed that Gaudentius was not strong enough to bear the strain such a diet imposed. The story, although it makes it difficult to know what the usual fasting rules were, does introduce the further distinction, celebrated in our time by Lévi-Strauss, between cooked and uncooked food. This, and further information on fasting rules, appears also in the *Life of Norbert*. A hermit there is described as being particularly assiduous about fasting. Winter and summer, he never ate more than once a day, except on Sundays and even then he only touched raw food. But one Lent he was tempted, and he became so hungry that he declared that he could not possibly fast at all and that he would certainly die, if he were made to give up even milk and cheese. To this he was told that it was not lawful for a layman to eat twice, nor for a child to have milk or cheese. This reply drove him to the brink of madness so that his other brethren conceded that he could eat twice, indeed as often as he liked, provided it was Lenten food and that he did not touch milk or cheese. At the time Norbert was away, but when he returned and learned of the affair he ordered that the man was to have no food whatsoever. After some days he was given bread and water and received it with relish.

As far as their habit was concerned, the hermits' greatest innovation was their departure from the custom of wearing black. Frequently they chose instead white or at least whitish colours, and those who wore grey, according to their critic, Pain Bolotin, thought themselves holiest of all. Ordericus Vitalis, too, has harsh words to say about those who 'as if to make a show of righteousness...reject black'.[38] There were, however, some hermits who did wear black, and even those who changed from white to black. The hermit-canons of Tournai, for example, were advised by the abbot of another eremitical foundation, Anchin, to become monks and wear black; as it was, their white habit made them seem like secular canons and they were therefore more tempted by them to return to the world. Some of the reasons for wearing white and for the kind of cloth they chose are also unexpected. The most renowned of the white monks, the Cistercians, wore undyed wool because this seemed to them the simplest possible habit and therefore in accordance with the provisions of Benedict's Rule. (It is interesting to notice that in their earliest years the Cistercian habit is also depicted as brown or grey; they must soon have decided to bleach it.) John Gualbert, on the other hand, noticed that some of his sheep were white and others black, and he decided that he would mix the wools so as to ensure that all his monks would wear the same colour. Other hermits were influenced by Scripture. Ailbert of Rolduc, for example, wore linen in imitation of the apostle James. St Norbert wore white because the angels who had appeared at the Resurrection had worn white, wool because it was the cloth of repentance, except in the sanctuary where he wore linen in imitation of the priests of the Old Testament. Robert of Arbrissel was criticised for his ragged and dishevelled looks – 'only a club was missing from the outfit of a lunatic'[39] – but many hermits seem to have gone out of their way not to be targets for this kind of attack. Their clothes were therefore simple but decent, holy in appearance rather than heretical, displaying what has been called, in another context, 'a carefully modulated shagginess'.[40]

7. Hermits, Reform and Preaching

EVEN without a Peter Damian, hermit and cardinal, to proclaim it, it would be hard to miss the connection between the eremitical and the papal reform movement. For hermits and Gregorians alike the church was to be purified, set free from corrupting institutions to return to the ways and customs of the early church. This much is clear from both papal and eremitical sources but it remains to be seen whether the movements overlapped in practice as well as in theory; the source of inspiration may have been the same but were the hermits in fact interested in issues, other than the monastic and canonical which directly affected them, that concerned Rome?

On the question of lay investiture, and of the relations between lay and ecclesiastical powers, the answer must be largely negative. St Norbert, for example, is said to have intervened to stop Innocent from ceding to Lothar rights of investiture, but this was not when he was a hermit but when he was archbishop of Magdeburg, moreover, the story is curiously reminiscent of the meeting at Liège between St Bernard, Innocent and Lothar. In France, two hermits, Robert of Arbrissel and Bernard of Tiron, were present at the council of Poitiers in 1100 called to pass judgement against the king for his liaison with Bertrada. They played – at least according to the *Life of Bernard* – a vital role in securing the sentence of excommunication against Philip, yet it cannot be said that there was anything specifically Gregorian about a pope censuring and condemning a king for matrimonial offences. More suggestive of a real alliance with Gregorian policies is the reference in Lampert of Hersfeld to the events of 1076: papal legates had been sent to Germany to organise the opponents of Henry IV and there came with them, sent by the pope, 'some laymen, who had forsaken their wealth and given themselves to a sparse and stringent life for God's sake'.[1] These laymen refused to have any contact with the supporters of Henry IV or with any who had attended the services of simoniac or married priests. But were they hermits or only lay agitators? Certainly, however, hermits were active in the papal schism of 1130. An anonymous poem records how they preached in Acquitaine in favour of Innocent. The difficulty here is to interpret the reasons for the schism and to decide what determined the alignment behind the two candidates, if it was caused by a Roman family feud, then those elsewhere in Europe who supported Innocent may only have been following the lead given by St Bernard. If, on the other hand, it was a conflict between two generations within the Sacred College, then the hermits must be listed among the 'new' reformers of the twelfth century as opposed to the 'old' Gregorians of the eleventh.

If such evidence is inconclusive, it is compensated for by what is known of the hermits' support of those aspects of the Gregorian reform which may loosely be termed moral: nicolaism and simony. Since the days of the early church a premium had been set on celibacy and decrees from the fourth century onwards aimed at enforcing it among the clergy. Although these were no longer by the eleventh century regarded as binding the concept of celibacy as an essential characteristic of the perfect Christian life had been kept alive by monks and nuns. Therefore its extension in the eleventh century to the secular clergy was in keeping both with the tradition and the decrees of the early church. It was also a practical measure since it dispelled the difficulties created by priests who had no inheritance other than church property with which to endow their sons. Its revival and the emotions it aroused are not difficult to understand. The battle over simony is more complex: an entrance fee is not after all an unusual concomitant to an election or a ceremony yet the reformers of the eleventh century felt with a passion perhaps comparable to that of the political reformers of the nineteenth century that purity in elections would have an immediate regenerative effect. The hermits proclaimed this as vehemently as anyone.

Romuald, according to Damian's *Life* of him, was the first to show by canon law that simony was a heresy;

> he reproved with particular severity those secular clerks who had been ordained with simony and he told them that unless they freely renounced the order which had been conferred on them then they were heretics and deserved to be damned. The clerks, on hearing so strange a sentiment, decided to kill him; for indeed in this region until the time of Romuald the custom was so firmly established that it was rare if the heresy of simony was ever considered a sin. Romuald therefore told the clerks 'Bring me the books of canons and you can tell me from those books whether what I say is true or not'. When the clerks had carefully consulted them they discovered their crime and lamented their mistake.[2]

A little later another Italian hermit, John Gualbert, took up the subject, and it was because of an incident of simony that he began his
life as a hermit. A new abbot had been appointed simoniacally for
his house of St Miniato and in protest John left. He went with a companion to Florence where he publicly denounced both the abbot and
the bishop who had sold him the post; the crowds who heard him are
described as being so incensed that they tried to kill him. Once
Vallombrosa was established John continued to fight simony. He
preached against it, he forbade any simoniacs or anyone ordained by
a simoniac to say Mass at Vallombrosa and he opposed the simoniac
bishop of Florence, Peter. His intransigence made him a central
figure in the ecclesiastical conflicts of Northern Italy. In 1068 a
monk of Vallombrosa undertook the ordeal of fire in order to prove
the Vallombrosan case against the bishop. The pope was taking too
long to act, but God himself would pronounce judgment and protect
his people. The crowd who had gathered at San Salvatore a Settimo
was addressed with these words:

> Brothers and sisters, we are doing this, as God is our witness, for
> the salvation of your souls, so that henceforth you may be safe
> from the leprosy of simony, which has now contaminated almost
> the whole world. And you know that the contagion of this leprosy
> is so great that in comparison with its enormity, other crimes are
> almost nothing.[3]

Parallels, even if less spectacular, may be found among the hermits of France. The *Rule of Grandmont* contains a special clause condemning simony – Bernard of Tiron and Bruno of Chartreuse, like
John Gualbert, fought simony early in their careers. Bernard found
that his abbot, if not guilty of simony as John's had been, was yet
prepared to enter into a transaction which Bernard considered had a
simoniacal character. Bernard, who was prior at the time, refused to
sanction the transaction. The abbot, in anger at being thus
thwarted, left his house and went on a crusade. The moral of the
story is duly underlined: the abbot was eaten by a lion and his fate
revealed to Bernard the same day. There was now a possibility that
Bernard himself might become abbot and it was to avoid this that he
escaped in secret to fulfil a long-felt wish to become a hermit. The
experience of Bruno of Chartreuse is similar. While he was head of
the cathedral school at Rheims the provost of the chapter confessed
that he had bought his post from the archbishop, Manasses. Bruno,

among other canons, supported the provost and with them was deprived of his goods and sent into exile. After several years of intrigue Manasses was deposed and Bruno elected to succeed him. Bruno declined, and shortly after began his pilgrimage in search of a hermitage. One hermit, Robert of Arbrissel, who had a foot in a simoniacal camp when avowedly a reformer, though not yet a hermit, remembered it even on his death bed when he confessed how he had been guilty of simony during the election of a bishop of Rennes. Another, Engeler by name, went even beyond the official teaching on the subject by proclaiming that the validity of the sacraments depended on the worthiness of the priest (and thereby earned himself a reproof from Marbod of Rennes).

For hermits, the most effective way of protesting against simony was by preaching. Eremitical leaders, as far as one can tell, always preached to their own disciples and very often to their immediate neighbourhood in return for alms. But there were also a number (though by no means all) who were ready to preach to a much wider audience, to travel far from their foundations to spread their teaching. Both Robert of Arbrissel and St Norbert were first and foremost preachers. When it was suggested that Norbert become abbot of St Martin in Laon he protested that this was not a suitable appointment since his function was to preach, and even after the foundation of Prémontré he continued to preach in both France and Germany. Robert of Arbrissel left his first foundation of La Roe because the canons complained he overcrowded it with those whom he had converted by his preaching and it was so that he could settle his ever-increasing number of disciples that he established Fontevrault. His fellow hermits in Brittany also felt themselves deeply committed to the task of preaching and did not allow their foundations to deter them from it. Vitalis of Savigny went as far as England.

The hermits have been seen primarily as penance preachers, the moral content of their sermons contrasted with the learned and philosophical teaching of an Abelard. This is only half the truth. If the hermits were not concerned with theological speculation it does not then follow that they were interested only in the salvation and repentance of the individual. This certainly was part of their mission, but it was not the whole of it. Their horizons were wider. Many of them felt passionately the need for reform throughout society and it was the aim of their preaching not only to move the people to confess their sins, but also to put new standards before them, and these not only for their own conduct, but also for the reorganisation of Christian society. They were interested in peace – both Norbert and Vitalis may be found ending blood feuds – and they were interested in restoring the church to, as they believed, its pristine condition. This was how they were led to preach on the subject of simony, and how too they took up such questions as clerical marriage, canonical reform, the state of the clergy, the holding by monasteries of tithes. That they were not only penance preachers was indeed a source of some of the grievances felt against them. Marbod of Rennes, for instance, in his letter to Robert of Arbrissel complained that instead of exhorting his audiences, composed largely of simple people, to lament their sins, he instead told them of the faults of their clergy.

A further and more fundamental question raised by their critics was how far the hermits had a right to preach at all since it was surely their place to live far from men and to be dead to the world. The same could, however, and sometimes was said of monks, with the backing of Jerome's comment that it was the task of the monk not to preach but to mourn. But those who in theory held such opinions might in practice contradict them; St Bernard is the obvious example. There was, moreover, a considerable school (it included Urban II) which saw no reason for denying monks the right to preach. The council of Chalcedon, it is true, had forbidden the practice but, wrote Bernold of Constance, the situation then was different. Monks at that time were laymen, now they took orders and they must in consequence be allowed the rights of the ordained. It is difficult to know, however, whether this was a reasoning the hermits shared. It does seem as if all those who publicly preached were priests, but this may have been no more than coincidence. When one of them, Bernard of Tiron, was challenged on the subject, he argued only that it was better for a preacher to be dead to the world; he took as his text Judges xv:1–16 and thereby compared himself with the jawbone of the dead ass which Samson had used with such effect. Yet for the hermits in their search for the *vita apostolica* there was in fact a clearer reason why they should preach. Christ had sent out his twelve disciples to do this, and further appointed another seventy for the purpose. Both Robert of Arbrissel and St Norbert took note of Christ's instructions that his disciples should take with them 'neither gold nor silver, nor brass...neither shoes nor staves' (Matthew x:9–10), and St Norbert, after he had solved a local feud, gave a sermon with a clear reference to the mission of the seventy (Luke x:5): 'brethren, when our Lord Jesus Christ sent his disciples to preach he gave them this command ... that whenever they entered a house they should first say "peace be to this house"'.[4] What is perhaps surprising is that it was only a number of hermits who felt the need to imitate this aspect of the apostles' lives; moreover, that none of them ever envisaged anything comparable to the plans of St Dominic. Rather than training their followers to preach, they established them in hermitages and there seem to have taught them the traditional doctrine of the eremitical life, that is, the desirability of avoiding contact with the secular world. Thus Norbert in his testament told his disciples that they must 'fear the company of men as a fish shuns dry land'.[5]

Before any hermit preached – and the same applied to monks – it was usual for him, or at least wise, to obtain a licence permitting him to do so. Whatever his theoretical right there were still problems which a licence must settle – where, for example, he was to preach and his relationship to the bishop of the diocese. Any unlicensed preacher might, moreover, *a priori* be held suspect since preaching was both the most likely and the most effective way of spreading heresy or sedition. Raoul of Mainz during the second crusade offended in this way by his preaching against the Jews. St Bernard found 'three things contemptible in him: unauthorized preaching, contempt for episcopal authority and incitement to murder'.[6] A hermit who was condemned for not having a licence was St Norbert; the council of Fritzlar in 1118 found him guilty of 'usurping the office of preaching'.[7]

St Norbert, after the passing of this sentence, went to St Gilles in Provence where Pope Gelasius then was, to appeal against it. In this he was successful. But shortly afterwards Gelasius died and Norbert felt he must apply to his successor Calixtus II for a renewal of the licence Gelasius had granted. He met Calixtus in the October of 1119 at the council of Rheims. But what passed between them is a matter of dispute. Not all historians would agree that Calixtus did renew the licence although this would seem, as Charles Dereine has argued, by far the most plausible interpretation both of the sources and of subsequent events. Others, for example Meersseman, believe that Calixtus in deference to the authority of the bishops because now they, too, were committed to the cause of reform, wanted to discontinue the practice of giving licences to preach since they put those who held them beyond episcopal jurisdiction. In either case, something must be said of the practice itself, and of the hermits' participation in it.

The first to hold such a licence seems to have been Wederic, monk of Ghent. He is known from the Affligem chronicle for it was he who converted the six knights who later founded that house. Wederic is described as a priest of noble birth who, with the backing of an apostolic licence, preached the word of God throughout Flanders. His mission is firmly set by the Affligem chronicler in the context of papal policies of the 1070s: this was the time when there was discord between pope and emperor, when the heresy of simony was rife and when priests had wives; Wederic was one of the few inspired by God to combat such a situation. The licensing of public preachers seems to have been initiated by Gregory VII as part of his reform programme and it was a scheme which Urban II continued. Urban is said to have heard Robert of Arbrissel speak at Angers in the spring of 1096 and to have been so impressed that he commissioned him to be a preacher. Urban also licensed Gaucher of Aureil and Bernard of Tiron. Bernard was 'to preach to the people, to hear confessions, to impose penances, to baptise, to go round the country and to fulfil all the duties of a public preacher'.[8] It is less certain that Peter the Hermit ever had such a licence. Whether or no, his preaching must still be differentiated from that of the other hermits since it was primarily concerned not with moral or penitential issues but with the crusade, a venture not regarded by all hermits with unequivocal enthusiasm.

Peter, to judge from Guibert de Nogent, was given a tumultuous reception by all who saw or heard him. Not all hermits were as welcome or as successful in their preaching. Peter Damian in the *Life of Romuald* recalls the limited results of Romuald's campaign against simony. Many bishops who had bought their sees came to him to confess their fault and made promises to resign their offices, but Damian doubts if any of them ever did: it would have been easier to bring a Jew to the faith. Other *Lives* tell of the crowds which came to hear the hermits, and how they heckled them – the wives of the clerks of Normandy, for example, are described as wanting to kill Bernard of Tiron when he talked to them of clerical celibacy.

Such scenes at the least gave publicity to the new papal policies, but it would be unlikely if this were their only effect. Although they might sometimes resent what was said there is yet evidence that the people wanted sermons; they asked Robert of Arbrissel to preach to them; they flocked to hear Bernard of Tiron – 'great crowds not only of hermits but also of the people rushed to him'.[9] Preaching (to

Guibert of Nogent at least) was of greater value than the cult of relics. A preacher should hold up a mirror to his audience so that they could see their inner selves. Ordericus Vitalis' description of Vitalis of Savigny's preaching is, in this context, interesting:

> Many multitudes journeyed to hear his words and, after hearing from his lips the shameful deeds that they had done in secret, withdrew in sorrow and confusion from his presence. Every rank was mortified by his true allegations, every crowd trembled before him at his reproaches; men and women alike blushed with confusion at his taunts. He laid bare vices and exposed them to the light, stabbing those who were aware of hidden faults with his pungent reproofs. So he often restrained haughty warriors and undisciplined rabbles, and caused wealthy ladies delicately clad in silk garments and fine lambskins to tremble when he attacked their sins with the sword of God's word, striking deeply into consciences defiled with filth and bringing terror with the rolling thunder of divine rebuke.[10]

The hermit-preachers, by the very nature of their way of life, by their poverty and their asceticism, might come much closer to the inhabitants of any locality than its own priests. This was a challenge and opportunity the hermits readily took up. They wanted to be not only seen but also heard, and understood. Language problems worried them. Pons de Léras and his followers, having reached Compostella, nonetheless did not settle there since 'it would not be profitable to stay among men of another tongue'.[11] When Gaucher of Aureil preached a funeral oration for his fellow-hermit Geoffrey of Chalard, he amazed those present because he would use no Latin at all, not even an opening verse of scripture. What is remarkable is that the hermits could combine this popular appeal with orthodoxy, that they defended and propagated new teaching without turning it into heresy. Not only that, they even, by their example and inspiration, for a time made heresy unnecessary. The heretics of the early eleventh century had too been seeking a holier life, based not on current institutions, but on the Gospel and the dividing line between their aspirations and those of the hermits could be very faint. In the case of Engelbald, hermit-founder of Hérival who for many years, because of his own unworthiness, would not celebrate Mass or communicate, it seems to have disappeared altogether. But Engelbald is an exceptional figure. The hermits kept generally to the side of orthodoxy because they respected authority and, in any case, authority was on their side. Popes and reforming bishops were prepared at this particular juncture to take the risks of allowing new foundations, new rules, itinerant preaching, for it was only in this way that the popular expectations roused by Gregorian reform could be both sustained and, at least for a time, contained.

8. Reactions to Hermits

ABOUT hermits there was a traditional view: their way of life was to be revered, they themselves were to be suspected because of the absence of any check over their activities. This criticism could not be applied with the same justice to the new communities of hermits since by living under a leader they were deliberately trying to avoid the 'arbitrary' self-regulated life. It must, however, be asked whether contemporaries recognised this difference and if they did how they judged the new movement.

Until a hermit of the new kind had been in the desert for some time and had gathered his disciples there may indeed have been few outside signs to distinguish him from a hermit of the traditional type. Where there was a group of hermits, however, contemporaries do seem to have felt there was something new and puzzling. The *Life* of Bernard of Tiron states that when the hermits first moved to Tiron the local inhabitants were so amazed by their poverty that they suspected that they must be Saracens who wanted to build underground caves from which they could spy on the people. Robert of Chaise-Dieu was apparently faced with a similar situation. Those who lived near Chaise-Dieu did nothing to help Robert and his followers. Hoped-for alms were not forthcoming, for the people thought the hermits must be insane to try to cultivate so barren a site. The biographers of Bernard of Tiron and of Robert may have recalled this hostility because it threw into relief the bravery of the hermits and the novelty of their seeking so comfortless a life, but there is nothing improbable in the hostility and the incredulousness itself. The entourage of Robert of Arbrissel undoubtedly caused alarm. Both Geoffrey of Vendôme and Marbod of Rennes wrote to him to warn him of the perils of allowing his men and women disciples to mix so freely. They did not accuse him personally of immorality, but rather of a new and not wholly salutary form of penance, contrary to all common sense, and if not dangerous to him, then to his disciples.

The difficulty of distinguishing in the first place between hermits of the new and of the traditional types and the subsequent bewilderment as to the former's aims may help to explain the inconsistencies that can be found in contemporary views, most notably in those of

Ivo, bishop of Chartres. Ivo wrote several letters to hermits, one to a certain Rainaud, two to Robert, and a letter to the monks of Colombs in which he was concerned with the recent activities of hermits. In the letter to Rainaud Ivo argued that by becoming a hermit Rainaud had done damage both to the community to which he previously belonged and to his own soul. He had broken his vows of profession and adopted an inferior form of life, inferior both in theory since it was a *vita voluntaria*, in other words there were no fixed rules, and in practice for experience had shown how often monks when they lived alone became degenerate. There were also positive reasons for the superiority of the coenobitic life; it gave opportunities for the exercise of charity towards fellow monks and for greater self-abnegation. To Robert, Ivo wrote first congratulating him on his wish to leave the world but telling him that he must, to fight the powers of evil, join a monastery. When he had gained experience then he could face the devil alone, but not before. Ivo pursued this subject in the second letter he wrote to Robert. If Robert starts from the beginning then he may reach the heights but let him beware lest by trying to start from the heights he should descend to the depths and let him be warned by men of their own generation not to incur such a disgrace. 'Grow your feathers in the nest before you take to the sky.'[1]

In his letter to the monks of Colombs Ivo expressed his disapproval of the preaching of certain hermits. The monks must not, he wrote, be led astray by hermits inciting them to leave their houses in protest against the ecclesiastical property they hold. He does not approve of their holding it but considers it preferable to be a coenobite living on tithes and oblations under a rule than to be a sarabaite leading an arbitrary life and accepting the alms of the poor. He concedes that there may be some virtue in the eremitical life, that it may be of use to those 'for whom solitude is paradise and the city a prison'.[2] The hermits he deplores are those who only pretend to love solitude and in reality spend their time wandering from place to place, deceiving the people by an appearance of piety.

These letters contain several different, even contradictory opinions on the eremitical life. In the letter to Rainaud the eremitical life is inferior to the coenobitical; when he writes to Robert, however, Ivo follows the teaching of the Benedictine *Rule* and here the eremitical life, while it is difficult and unsuitable for novices, is yet superior; in the letter to the monks of Colombs his praise for it is much more grudgingly given. What then can be said of Ivo's attitude to the eremitical life beyond the fact of his inconsistency? The hermits he wrote to or about belonged almost certainly to the new eremitical movement. Rainaud has been identified by Dom Morin as a canon of Soissons and later the founder of an oratory in the forest of Melinais. Robert is thought by some historians to be Robert of Arbrissel. The monks of Colombs clearly belonged to the militant wing of the movement. Yet the terms in which Ivo wrote in these letters of the eremitical life, the lack of companions and of a rule, make it seem unlikely that he could have known of the change in its character. Moreover, when Ivo came face to face with the hermits of the movement it was not as their critic but rather as their ally. He witnessed the foundation of La Roe, he secured for Bernard and his disciples the site of Tiron.

In the same way it would be a mistake to gauge Marbod of Rennes' attitude to the eremitical movement only in terms of his letter to Robert of Arbrissel. The letter was critical of Robert's dress and appearance, of his manner of preaching, of his organisation of his disciples. But Robert's way of life was in fact particularly likely to arouse anxiety, and there were also special reasons why Marbod, as Robert's former master at Rennes, should have felt the need to protest. Marbod was not in principle unfriendly to the eremitical movement. His sympathetic biography of Robert of Chaise-Dieu makes this clear.

The bishops were in general the hermits' most consistent supporters. Robert of Arbrissel himself was not short of friends among the episcopate: Baudry of Dol wrote his *Life*, the bishops of Angers, Poitiers, Angoulême, and the archbishop of Bourges were among his patrons, and Robert in 1109 placed Fontevrault and any other foundations in Poitiers under Peter of Poitiers' protection. In Grenoble, bishop Hugh is said to have been so attracted by the Carthusians that Bruno had to remind him not to neglect his diocesan duties. When Bruno left for Italy Hugh himself founded the hermitage of Chalais. In England, episcopal support for the new hermits was remarkable not only in the 1130s at the time of the foundation of Fountains, but also a generation earlier when hermits had arrived from the south to bring back monasticism to its first shrines.

Bishops, moreover, tried to tempt hermits into their sees. Burchard of Utrecht, for example, offered Ailbert a finer site than he had at Rolduc if he would leave Liège for Utrecht. The offer failed to tempt

Ailbert since he feared that acceptance could compromise his ideal of poverty. The relations between Bartholomew of Laon and St Norbert were more fruitful. According to Herman of Laon it was Bartholomew who made sure that Norbert gained the audience he wanted with Calixtus at the council of Rheims and it was to Bartholomew and Burchard of Cambrai, according to the *Life of Norbert*, that the pope entrusted Norbert's health; only the year before Burchard had looked after Norbert when he fell ill on his way back to Germany after his visit to Gelasius. To avoid a repetition of the perils of this journey Norbert was persuaded to winter in Laon, but there is no evidence that he had any intention at that moment of staying there permanently. This idea would seem to have come from Bartholomew, who saw the value of keeping Norbert in his diocese. To this end he tried first to secure his appointment as abbot of St Martin, then, when this had failed, he offered him various sites where he could start his own community. When Norbert had agreed to his plan, Bartholomew both secured the ground he wanted and added to it. This role of Bartholomew's in the founding of Prémontré did not pass unrecognised; a Premonstratensian obituary calls him 'the founder of our order'.[3]

The importance of this episcopal support in the new movement cannot be overestimated; the hermits, often newcomers to the diocese in question, relied to a great extent on the bishops' goodwill. That they got it, as has been already suggested, may help to explain the orthodoxy of the movement. Without it, they could have been, like Durand de Huesca at the end of the century, driven into heresy. For they needed the bishop for purposes of benediction and consecration, sometimes to give them land, to confirm their leader and their way of life. The bishop might also help hermits to decide about the form their lives should take and later, on the customs to adopt. As we have seen, the hospital of Flône was founded on the advice of the bishop of Verdun, Affligem on the advice of the archbishop of Cologne. When the hermits wanted to become monks they then consulted the bishop of their diocese, Gerard of Cambrai, since in the words of the Charter he granted in 1086, 'they were laymen and relied greatly on our advice'.[4]

The kind of sites the hermits wanted and their belief in manual labour made them pleasing also to certain lay patrons. Pons de Léras, who had refused the first site offered to him in favour of a remote piece of woodland, was subsidised by his patron Arnold of Ponte because

Arnold was afraid that without help the foundation would collapse and 'the place would again become a wilderness'.[5] But the hermits had at times finer sites and they might then have difficulty if, for instance, they were in the gift of more than one person – this was the case at Savigny – or alternatively from the donor's heirs. The hermits of Chaumouzey, for instance, were long troubled by the claims of the brother of their patron. Their right to the allod he had given them was upheld both by the Duke and by the bishop of Toul but they had nonetheless to pay compensation to the brother before he would confirm the gift and cease molesting the hermits. There is, however, little positive evidence to suggest that the hermits were ever seriously hindered through the unwillingness of landowners to help them; it must be remembered too that some of the hermits were themselves landowners and could therefore endow their own hermitages. But this takes no account of the hermitages which may, from lack of support, have vanished without a trace. There are several indications of slow and precarious beginnings, at Fountains, for example, and at Cîteaux. At St Laurent, a house of regular canons, possibly of eremitical origin, there were after fifteen years 'only seven brethren, four canons and three laymen, and they had not yet enough to maintain a plough'.[6] In these cases many donations were to come, but it cannot always have been so.

The popes usually intervened in the hermits' foundations only when they were well established. They then gave bulls of confirmation and often too they showed their approval of the new houses by granting them exemption from the payment of tithes on lands they themselves had cultivated. There are, however, instances of papal support for the movement in its earlier stages. Stephen of Grandmont before he left Italy had his plan to found a hermitage approved by the pope; Urban II, Calixtus and Gelasius gave licences to hermit-preachers; Paschal made Conon of Arrouaise cardinal bishop of Preneste; Urban II called Bruno of Chartreuse to the curia to be his advisor. Papal legates too may be found acting on the hermit's behalf. They were present at the foundation of Sauve Majeure and La Roe and it was a papal legate who confirmed Stephen of Obazine as the leader of his community. In Italy where there was more chance of actual meetings between popes and hermits it might be the hermits who were the unwilling party. The *Life* of John Gualbert tells how pope Leo once asked to see Gualbert. Gualbert was ill – 'he would not and could not go'.[7] Leo therefore ordered that Gualbert be carried to him in his bed, but Gualbert then prayed for some other reason which would prevent him from having to go, and on the appointed day there was a storm.

The hermits' chief opponents may be found among the black monks whose supremacy they were threatening, and among the secular priests who resented their preaching. To the black monks the reforms of the hermits seemed presumptuous and unnecessary. It was to them unreasonable to try to revive the austerities of early monasticism. They saw the first centuries of the church not as a golden era, but as a time of persecution and suffering. Experience had since taught them forms of monasticism they considered both satisfactory and practical and they saw no reason for abandoning these in favour of new and harsher observances. Thus the monks of Molesme, according to Ordericus Vitalis, told those of their house who wanted to revive the practice of manual labour that it was an ancient custom for the peasants to do this, that they themselves were exempt from it because of their concentration on the *Opus Dei* and that as long as the monks of Cluny and of Tours lived in this fashion they did not intend to depart from the traditions of their forefathers. The same kind of arguments were used also by those who regretted that they had ever been attracted by the new forms of the religious life. Two Carthusians complained to Hugh of Lincoln;

> Wretch, you have deluded us... You have forced us to lurk among beasts and thorns, as if there were not places of monastic retirement in the world. The whole land is full of communities of monks, and the mutual support provided by the communal life provides us with a sufficiently good example of religious perfection. The yoke of this new law which you tell us must be borne as if all Christians everywhere would be damned except the Carthusians ... is almost unendurable in this world.[8]

Such tensions were to reach their height in the mid-twelfth century, but the beginnings of the conflict may be found much earlier, while the hermits were first establishing their communities. In this they were occasionally helped by black monks; thus it was on land belonging to Guarinus of Cuxa that Romuald started his first community. But more often the black monks were hostile. Bernard of Tiron, for example, had difficulty in finding a site because of Cluniac opposition; there were disputes between Robert of Arbrissel and the abbey of St Paul of Cormericus, between Affligem and the abbey of Lobbes about land. In England, the opposition of Geoffrey, abbot of St

Mary's, to Richard and his reform party was such that it caused reverberations throughout the country. It can be noted how often in these and in comparable cases bishops intervened on the hermits' behalf. Thus Peter of Poitiers gave judgement against St Paul's in favour of Fontevrault; Henry of Liège secured the land for Affligem which Lobbes had claimed and Thurstan, archbishop of York, gave unstinting support to Richard of St Mary's.

The theoretical objections to hermits' preaching and the kind of response they might in fact receive from their audiences have been mentioned elsewhere. Here something can perhaps be said of the more particular problem of the reaction of the secular clergy. Clearly, when the hermits' preaching was successful they resented it. This can be shown both from the letter of Marbod of Rennes to Robert of Arbrissel – Robert, according to Marbod, was depriving priests of their parishioners and of their livelihood – and also from the *Life* of Geoffrey of Chalard. Geoffrey, when he was looking for a site where he could live as a hermit, received support from a local priest, but once he was established Geoffrey's popularity both alarmed and angered the priest. He was afraid that his parishioners would no longer give him their offerings and he therefore, with the backing of an archdeacon of Limoges, lodged a complaint with the bishop of Périgueux (the see of Limoges was vacant at the time) claiming that Geoffrey was usurping the 'cure of souls' and asking for him to be silenced. The bishop refused the request. The *Life* points out that in this way Geoffrey fulfilled the prophecy of a Flemish hermit who had lived before him in the same place, but had been chased away by priests. As he fled he threatened that although he, as a layman, had no power to resist them yet he would be followed by one whom they would be unable to defeat.

The fullest literary attack on the new hermits may be found in a poem by Pain Bolotin, identified through Ordericus Vitalis' mention of him. He himself, more tolerant than many black monks, wrote of the new monks: 'In my opinion voluntary poverty, contempt of the world and true religion inspire the greater part of them, but many hypocrites and plausible counterfeiters are mingled with them as tares with wheat'. Their hypocrisy had, he said, been admirably exposed by a canon of Chartres, Pain Bolotin, 'subtly and at length'.[9]

To Pain, the false hermits were a new menace, troublesome throughout the country. They were wolves in sheeps' clothing, and there was absolutely no good in them. They would not stay in their cloisters, but wandered around in towns, some in long black tunics, others wearing white and the 'holiest' in greyish colours. They were immoral, but pretended to be of the highest integrity; they were rich and insatiably avaricious, but feigned great poverty. They criticised the clergy, but their own lives were much more scandalous. Nonetheless, they succeeded in deceiving both the people and the bishops; in this way they themselves became bishops and lived thereafter in the greatest of ease and comfort. They were, concluded Pain, a plague like the frogs of Egypt, a sign that the end of the world was near. The white they wore was not a symbol of holiness, rather it represented the pallor of death.

However, Pain made a reservation: there were also good hermits who should be esteemed. But he unfortunately gave only one example of a good hermit and nothing is known of the kind of life he led. It is nonetheless clear that Pain resented in particular the preaching of the hermits and that he believed their rightful place to be 'in woods and forests'. This could perhaps mean that Pain admired only traditional hermits, and that to him all new hermits were false hermits – Ordericus mentions them and so do the new hermits themselves – but there are passages, especially at the end of Pain's poem, which would be difficult to understand if it was only this group and not the whole eremitical movement which Pain disliked. The false hermits had, he wrote, been attacking traditional monasticism for the last thirty-two years; by this he seems to have meant from about 1100. They had organised themselves into a rival order, they boasted of its lay character, they claimed that the Benedictines were lazy and greedy, but they were to Pain in no way worthy of the esteem the Benedictines once had held: 'we all know this newness of religion. It started thirty-two years ago and already the order of the black monks is held in contempt'.[10] From there it was no distance to the conflict between Cluniacs and Cistercians.

There can be no doubt that many observers found such polemics and 'intolerable wrangling' both damaging and embarrassing and did what they could to encourage tolerance. We have already mentioned (in the section on manual labour) the tract known as *The Orders and Callings of the Church*. It is time now to look at the writer's general analysis for his perspective is of particular relevance. First he describes 'traditional' hermits, those who live alone or with a few others; then monks and canons judged in the light of the new eremitical principles – whether or not they live close to men, the strictness of their discipline. The writer makes it clear that his aim is 'to demonstrate what is good in each calling' and not 'to carp at the deeds of others with a biting pen',[11] 'I am not eager to blame anyone for his order, but I desire to show that, though they live differently, they aspire from one beginning to one end which is Christ.'[12] Nonetheless, in a passage of great magnanimity the author shows how hard it was not to feel that the old orders – his own included – were now second-best:

> It ought not to seem a serious matter to anyone if I judge a man who takes up a greater labour for Christ to be nearer the inner sanctuary, or if I say that he is a little more like Christ than I in carrying His cross, he who has taken hold of a greater part of that most pious burden than I have. Since they watch, fast, labour and brave the elements more than I, and, to come to more important things, are among those who are more humble and poor before Christ, I regard these men bowed under that most pious burden before all eyes as higher and stronger and I see myself, having put my shoulders with them under that burden and positioned my hands and stretched out my arms in a more lowly fashion, in order being weaker to do what I can.[13]

Beryl Smalley has pointed out how to both Pain Bolotin and the writer of *The Orders and Callings of the Church* anything that can be called 'new' is at best to be treated with suspicion and as likely as not will be downright bad. To Pain, 'novelty is not only bad in itself; it prophesies something worse'.[14] *The Orders and Callings of the Church* goes out of its way to prove by the use of every possible biblical precedent that none of the orders described really is new. These were arguments familiar and acceptable to the hermits themselves, yet paradoxically it is from the orders they founded that 'the breakthrough on the question of religious novelties'[15] was to come; to the Premonstratensian, Anselm of Havelberg, writing in the 1150s novelty was both healthy and vital for the development of the church. St Norbert himself was praised in his *Life* for preaching 'a new type of life on earth'.[16]

9. The Adoption of an Order and Customs

EREMITICAL communities if they prospered were, as has been seen, organised under a leader whose commands, if not beyond criticism, were yet regarded as both necessary and authoritative. A certain recognisable pattern was imposed on the hermits' lives by their observances of the offices of the church but in other respects their routine diverged greatly from that of established religious houses. Their poverty, their asceticism, their practice of manual labour in particular were traits which marked them out as different. In general the hermits seem to have been able to forge this new way of life fairly peacefully among themselves. In some communities there were quarrels as to both means and aims but it seems as if the leaders had more often to try to give shape to religious aspirations than to reconcile conflicting schemes. But the hermits were seldom content to have simply established a working community. They were not sure that to live in obedience only to a superior was a sufficient guarantee against the pitfalls of an arbitrary life. They felt uneasy at having no recognised status within the church, at having to depend on the spoken word rather than the written rule and they felt worried about the permanence of their ideals, how to ensure the continuity of their settlements. Their anxieties are succinctly expressed in the *Life* of Stephen of Obazine: 'they wanted to belong to an order authorised by the Church, so that, in the absence of their masters, there would remain to them the unfailing authority of a written law'.[1]

The decision to join an order is often presented as coming both from the leader and from the community together. In some cases, however, the initiative was definitely taken either by one or the other. St Norbert's followers are described as being content to obey his words and to feel no need for other guidance; it was left, therefore, to Norbert, afraid that otherwise his foundation would have no sure future, to persuade them that without an order and a rule and the laws of the Fathers they could not fully observe the commands of the Gospels. There were in contrast leaders who felt reluctant to relinquish the independence of their communities. This seems to have been so with Geoffrey of Fontaine les Blanches. His disciples urged

him constantly to join some order – they did not mind which – but
he would give them no reply. Then, when he was ill, they seized their
chance, begging him to make some decision in case he should die
leaving their future unsettled. If he did not want to give his house
over to black monks, surely, they argued, Savigny must be acceptable: to which he replied 'if you want to send, send: and they seized
the words from his mouth'.[2] At Gâstines, in Tours, on the other
hand, the community was split. Christian, later a monk of l'Aumône,
was the first to consider the possibility of joining the Cistercians. He
discussed the plan with his fellow hermits but could not gain
unanimous support. It was agreed therefore that those who wanted
to become Cistercians might, with the blessing of those who remained, be free to do so. In time the leader of Gâstines himself followed
Christian's suggestion.

It might seem, perhaps, as if the hermits, in this wish to belong to
an established order, were defeating their own ends, were retracing
the steps which had led them to the desert; the price of a secure place
within the church was surely the acceptance of the religious mores
they had originally rejected. One group, the Grandmontese, did in
fact carry such arguments to their conclusion, refusing to acknowledge the necessity of an order, denying, to some extent out of humility, but also as a matter of principle, that they were either monks,
canons or hermits. The Gospel was to be their only rule. There were
also three communities – Fonte Avellana, Camaldoli and La Grande
Chartreuse – which never embraced, as did the other hermits of
the new movement, the full communal life and where the organisation was too novel for it to fit into any existing pattern. These
communities excepted, the hermits were content to become either
Benedictine or Augustinian; there were several reasons why they
believed they could do so without betraying either the theory or the
practice of their ideals. Their decisions well illustrate the twelfth
century concern (recently examined by Colin Morris and C.W.
Bynum) not only for individuality but also for models, the belief that
'through imitation of [good men] we may be reformed to the likeness
of a new life ... In them the form of the likeness of God is clear and
therefore when we are imprinted by these things through imitation,
we are also shaped in the image of the same similitude'.[3]

Those hermits who became Benedictine argued that if the *Rule of
Benedict* was properly kept, that is to say 'to the letter', then to follow
it was to return to the ways of the early church, even to the teaching

of the Gospels. The persistence with which these hermits announced their intention to follow only the *Rule*, and to have no glosses, gives the impression that this was a possible programme. In practice, however, pure Benedictinism was to prove a reformers' illusion. It is well known how the Cistercians evolved the *Carta Caritatis* and the *Instituta* to supplement the Benedictine *Rule*. Other communities which had started with the same aim as the Cistercians fared no better in fulfilling it. It is difficult to know exactly how this happened. Richard, as prior of St Mary's in York, was able to give to his abbot, Geoffrey, in writing, a clear account of his plans for reform, how there would be full observance of the Benedictine *Rule* and how this would mean the renunciation of tithes and that monks should live instead by the work of their own hands. Faced with Geoffrey's opposition Richard and those who supported him left St Mary's and with the help of the archbishop of York, Thurstan, they founded the hermitage which was soon to become the Cistercian abbey of Fountains. Their request to join Clairvaux, however fruitful, was nonetheless an admission of failure, of loss of confidence. The hermits were replacing the customs of St Mary's with the customs of Cîteaux. They had not, as they had intended, succeeded in following only the *Rule of Benedict* because they had found that this demanded powers of interpretation they were not prepared to use:

> That winter, as they huddled under their skins, they talked among themselves about their status, how they should live and under what discipline. For it did not seem to them to be right to trust their own whims and intuition, lest they should be tricked and deceived.[4]

Despite this need for customs the hermit-Benedictines clung to their notion of the full observance of the *Rule of Benedict*; yet in reality it was the adoption of, and development of customs which gave to their communities their originality, which made them markedly different from Benedictines of non-eremitical stock.

Much the same can be said of those hermits who adopted the *Rule of Augustine*; it was customs rather than the *Rule* itself which determined the character of each community. The Augustinian order was itself, however, a reformers' creation, the outcome of attempts to replace the *capitula* of Aix by a much more rigorous concept of the canonical life, one which emphasised the *vita apostolica*, the need for poverty. The ideals of these reformers and of the hermits were therefore closely allied and this was not only a matter of coincidence:

many of the first communities of regular canons were formed either
by hermits or as a result of their teaching. Although a connection
between Cluniac influence and the rise of the regular canons has
often been alleged more recent work has shown that, on the contrary,
Cluny played little, if any, part in the beginnings of the new movement; the initiative came rather from eremitical milieux; regional
studies by continental scholars concerned with unravelling the
origins of eleventh- and twelfth-century foundations continue to
show how true this is. Therefore some account of the beginnings of
the Augustinian order must be given to show how the hermits came
both to join it and to influence its formation.

The movement of regular canons is difficult to trace since working
at the same time there were reformers who wanted to rescind the
legislation of 817 and those who wanted to restore it and both
justified their measures in the name of the common and regular life.
Only direct references to the question of private property make it
possible to distinguish between the two schools, and these are often
lacking. What is clear from the debates surrounding it is that the
papal decree of 1059 in favour of the canons regular was not intended to introduce an innovation but to give support to a spontaneous
movement that was already underfoot. Hildebrand, leading the
discussions, spoke of certain clerks both in Rome and in areas
specially attached to her who had adopted the full communal life,
had given up private property and were trying to live 'according to
the example of the primitive church'.[5] These clerks had, he claimed,
been dissuaded from their renunciation of private property in the
name of the rule drawn up in the reign of the emperor Louis. They
had therefore been made guilty of apostasy and Hildebrand urged
that something be done to strengthen them in their former resolve.

Hildebrand did not mention by name any of the communities he
was trying to help, but he said they had been established for some
time. It is therefore possible that they included those founded under
the guidance of Romuald and of John Gualbert. Their preaching in
favour of the common life for clerks is among the earliest evidence
there is of canonical reform in this period. It must, however, be admitted that Peter Damian's *Life* of Romuald is not absolutely clear
on this subject: 'the holy man established many houses of canons and
taught clerks who had been living in a secular fashion, like laymen,
to obey priors and to live together as a community'.[6] Damian's own
passionate advocacy of the movement of regular canons perhaps

makes it probable that he would not have wanted it remembered had his hero worked for anything less, but since the passage is silent on the crucial problem of property this can be no more than a hypothesis. With John Gualbert there is none of this ambiguity. His first biographer, Andrew of Strumi, praises John for having established the apostolic life among clerks and he makes it clear what he means by this by describing how lamentable was the condition before: 'Which congregation of clerks was leading a common life? Which clerk was not intent on his own and his paternal property? ... which one was not either married or living with a woman?'[7]

The first evidence for hermit-canons in France is less certain, but it is probable that here too, as in Italy, hermits were among the pioneers of the movement. The possibility of there being a group of hermits who later became canons at Bénévent in the Limousin as early as 1028 has already been mentioned; something has also been said of the problems concerning the origins of St Ruf. At Mont Salvy in St Flour hermit-canons may be found c.1066, and at Pebrac in Clermont, c.1062. In Liège, the earliest and most celebrated houses of regular canons, Flône, St Gilles, Neufmoustier and Rolduc were all four founded by hermits. One of the oldest houses in England, perhaps even the oldest, St Botolph's, Colchester, was first composed of a group of priests living together in search of a rule, yet it must be said, as for St Ruf, that there is no positive evidence for supposing it to be eremitical. But both Nostell and Llanthony are early examples of houses of hermit-canons.

There is a clear connection between the new hermits and the first Augustinian canons; there is also this similarity between the two movements that although – or perhaps since – they were both revolutionary they felt they needed the testimony of the Fathers to support their reforms, thus the hermit-monks claimed to be the true interpreters of the *Rule of Benedict*, while the hermit-canons helped the emergence of the *Rule of St Augustine*, a text which, in the form most commonly found, added little but authority to the canonical movement. There was indeed one version of the rule, the *Ordo Monasterii*, which did prescribe detailed regulations for a community, but it was not a version that was widely known and its authenticity was doubted. The more usual text was composed of two parts, the *Regula Prima*, a dissertation on apostolic poverty, and the *Regula Tertia*, a masculine version of the second part of Augustine's letter to his sister which contained only general directives on the running of a community.

The *Rule of Augustine*, therefore, in its usual form, provided those hermits who adopted it with little more than an ending of their, to them, anomalous position in the church. This in itself they considered to be a sign of obedience. In the chronicle of Chaumouzey, for example, it is recorded that they would adopt the *Rule of Augustine* – 'it pleased all of us whom the love of poverty, the ever aspiring nurse of virtue drove on to conduct life according to the Institutes of St. Augustine under the canonical habit and to expect from God the prize of supreme remuneration from consummate obedience under regular discipline'.[8] This passage might suggest that the hermits had now a definite way of life, but it is clear from subsequent deliberations that what it meant was that they had a recognised status. It was only later that they began to feel the need for 'laws and customs' and that they therefore applied to St Ruf for instruction as to how canons should live.

The interval that elapsed at Chaumouzey between the adoption of an order and of customs was probably longer than in most communities, but it underlines that in those cases where the two steps were taken simultaneously – for example, when a group of hermits became Cistercian – they were, nonetheless, logically distinct. The problem of which order to join could be solved without any thought of the customs that might thereafter be followed. In most cases the hermits hesitated between becoming monks or canons but they might also consider making permanent their eremitical status. The necessity of this last step may seem strange, but because the hermits did not regard their eremitical life as definitive, it was as great a decision to become officially eremitical as it was to become monastic or canonical. This is made clear in the *Life of Norbert* where Norbert and his followers in their search for an order are advised by many bishops and abbots to become hermits, anchorites or Cistercians.

Norbert's final decision to make his community Augustinian was made for a reason that seems almost trivial. According to the *Life of Norbert* his chief consideration was the fact that he and many of his followers had earlier been professed as canons – albeit seculars – and he did not want them to have to desert this way of life. It was thus a matter of chance rather than of design that Prémontré became canonical and not monastic or eremitical. It is striking how often similarly fortuitous factors proved decisive. In a large number of cases the hermits had no marked preference for one order over another;

their uncertainties and the circumstantial reasons which might govern their final choice emerge clearly from the *Lives*. The account in the *Life* of Pons de Léras, for example, gives an indication of the informality of the discussions, of the hermits' doubts and dilemmas and the way they therefore tended to rely on institutions that had already acquired reputation and fame:

> An argument therefore broke out among them as to which order was the greater, some praising the Cistercian, others the Carthusians, some even saying that it would be good to build a house for nuns. Then it was decided to lay the whole matter before the Carthusians and to leave the decision to them.[9]

Another solution was for the hermits to seek the help of a local bishop. The hermits of Obazine, for example, who had hesitated for some time between the possibility of becoming monks or canons regular, chose the former largely on the advice of bishop Aimeric of Clermont; Geoffrey of Chalard made his community Augustinian under the guidance of Raynaud, bishop of Périgueux.

Once they had chosen their order, the next concern of the hermits was to find suitable customs. Some preferred to codify their own and might do so with such success – as, most notably, in the cases of Cîteaux and Prémontré – that the customs themselves gave rise to new orders. It might take years, even many decades, before such customs were written down, but while this implies a long process of evolution there are instances where the initiative of the first leader can yet be seen. John Gualbert, as soon as he was officially appointed abbot of Vallombrosa, is described as making a careful study of the Benedictine *Rule* and his biographer gives an account of the provisions he thereby made. Shortly before his death Robert of Arbrissel called an assembly of ecclesiastical notables and in their presence and with their advice – for example, on the constitutional propriety of having a woman who had been married as an abbess – he drew up statutes for Fontevrault. A similar attempt to provide his disciples with definitive customs was made by Stephen of Grandmont. According to his *Life* he spent four days telling them of the rules and precepts they should observe, on the fifth day he died.

There were, however, also leaders who, having chosen an order, preferred to abandon their own practices and to adopt the customs of another house. There are a number of possible reasons why this proved an attractive alternative. To begin with, not all leaders can have

wanted to be also law-makers. The problems of being in charge of
followings probably larger than they had ever imagined were great
enough without adding further responsibilities. Nor can the leaders
always have had sufficient ability or experience to legislate. Many of
them were laymen or secular clerks with little or no previous experience of the workings of a religious community, of how monks and
canons actually lived. The borrowing of customs, moreover, often
implied affiliation to the house concerned and this gave to the
daughter house not only constitutional but also some degree of financial security. This is never explicitly given as a reason for affiliation,
but it would be strange if the hermits did not at some point consider
it. The possibilities of famine and the uncertainties of donations
made the hermits' settlements precarious. The first years of Fountains, for example, were marked by extreme poverty, and the hermits
were forced to consider moving elsewhere. Gifts from a deacon at
York finally made this unnecessary and but for these the one solution
to the hermits' needs would have been to leave England to go to the
site which Bernard of Clairvaux, the house to which they were affiliated, had offered them. There are also cases where the hermits
did in fact change sites on the advice of, and with the help of, their
new masters: thus the hermits of Mont-Saint-Martin under the aegis
of their Premonstratensian instructors moved their community
nearer a river. It also seems likely that a house might be reluctant to
have connections with a hermitage it felt could become an economic
burden. This is possibly the explanation of the relations between
Arrouaise and Vicogne. Wido of Vicogne had asked for canons from
there to teach his followers their customs. The canons came but when
they saw the site they were afraid it could never be cultivated and
they returned home.

The hermits chose which customs to adopt in much the same way
as they chose their order. The essential condition was that they
should come from a house recently established and based on the new
principles; thereafter the hermits let themselves be guided by the
reputation a house had gained and by the advice of ecclesiastical
notables, in particular of their bishop. Thus the hermits of Affligem
with the support of bishop Gerard of Cambrai sought instruction in
the monastic way of life from Anchin – 'because of its renown, it was
more famous than other monasteries both for fraternal charity and
the rigours of holy religion'.[10] Likewise, the hermits of Chaumouzey
with letters of introduction from Pibo of Toul asked for Augustinian

customs from the house of St Ruf. The decisive factor was often geographical since it was clearly more practical to have instruction from a nearby house than from one many miles away. This did not always leave the hermits with much choice. Dalon, which instructed the monks of Obazine, is described as being the only one of its kind in the district – 'there was no reformed house in that region then except Dalon'.[11] In some areas, however, there was no suitable foundation at all. Gaucher of Aureil, who was uncertain about both the order and the customs for his community, had to go from the Limousin as far as Avignon since 'in his own province there was not then a hermit or a white monk to be found'.[12] He then chose to live for two years with the canons of St Ruf.

The hermits' lack of preconceived ideas about which order to join and the customs to adopt worked both ways; sometimes it meant that they chose quickly and at random, at other times it entailed years of doubts, hesitations, experiments. Odo of Tournai first adopted the *Rule of Augustine* since the liturgy, the food and the habits of canons seemed to him 'more tolerable'[13] than those of monks, but he changed after two years to the *Rule of Benedict* since he was advised that this would place his followers further from the world. The search of Stephen of Obazine for a settlement for his community shows how long protracted an affair it could be. He made it a matter of policy to visit nearby houses to learn about their way of life and then, because he had heard of its fame, he undertook the long journey from the Limousin to Chartreuse. He there asked for advice from the prior Guy, 'as to which way of religion he should choose'.[14] Guy told him that he could not himself accept Obazine as a daughter house since by Carthusian standards it was already too large but he recommended him to apply to Cîteaux which, as a coenobitic institution, was suitable 'both for the many and the few'.[15] Stephen did not immediately act on this suggestion. He seems to have been greatly impressed by Chartreuse and perhaps felt that if he could not join, he could at least try to imitate her, for he returned to Obazine and began the building of a church dedicated to the Virgin, in imitation of the Carthusians. He did not, however, consider this a sufficient solution, and in the early 1140s he returned to the problem of finding an order. The main question this time was whether his followers wanted to be monks or canons regular; as has been mentioned, they chose the former with the help of the bishop of Clermont. But Stephen's biographer explains that they still knew little or nothing of the monastic way of life: 'although perfected in religion, yet as monks they were simple'.[16] Monks therefore came from Dalon, a foundation of Gerard de Salles', to teach them their customs but they did so with such haste that they were much resented and Stephen had some difficulty in calming his offended disciples. Nor does Stephen himself seem to have been satisfied. Six years later he reverted to Guy's suggestion and went to Cîteaux to find out whether such an arrangement would be acceptable. With the help of Eugenius III, who was then staying at Cîteaux, the request for affiliation was granted and Cistercian instructors sent to Obazine. This time it was Stephen who objected to their lessons. He had as a hermit been adamant that under no circumstances should meat be eaten and he found it hard to accept the Benedictine ruling that some should be allowed to the sick.

Stephen of Obazine's experiences show how, although affiliation and the adoption of customs might bring security, there were also problems, a reluctance after a time of self-rule to obey commands imposed by others, to give up one's own usages for the sake of conformity. The *Life of Stephen* in particular shows this, but there are signs of it too in other houses. The monks of Anchin, for example, were unpopular at Affligem and it was finally Fulgence, a former monk of Verdun, who composed the needed customs. Such friction helps to explain how, although by 1150 so many hermits had sought affiliation, there were yet enough independent houses both to impress and to trouble contemporaries: 'Why should there be so many novelties in the Church of God? Why should so many orders rise up in her? Who can count so vast a number of clerks' orders?'[17]

10. The End of the Hermitages

To attempt a detailed analysis of the customs finally adopted by the various groups of hermits which have been mentioned would be to go too far into monastic and canonical history, but some account may perhaps be given of their character, of how the eremitical communities developed, of how, and for how long, they differed from the more conventional houses of monks and canons regular.

It has already been mentioned that the inspiration behind the campaign for regular canons was to a large extent eremitical, yet in the official plans an element of this inspiration was lacking, namely the wish for austerity. Neither the decree of 1059 nor Gregory VII's rule made any great ascetic demands and indeed it was this moderation that finally came to characterise the movement. It also came to be accepted that regular canons both could and should exercise the 'cure of souls'; in other words, undertake pastoral work. But many hermit-canons, at least for some years, chose to remain outside these developments, or if they conformed to one, then to resist the other. Thus the hermit-canons of Chaumouzey who had adopted the moderate customs of St Ruf did not at first serve the parish of Chaumouzey, preferring to give the cure to a secular priest.

Hérival, in Toul, was particularly faithful to its eremitical origin. There is no evidence that the clerks here had any parish duties and indeed it sounds from the rule as if this would have been impossible since during Lent the clerks were not even allowed outside the cloister. Their life was one of extreme asceticism and simplicity. Apart from having no private property – and care was taken lest they should become too attached to the tools they used for work – they were not as a community allowed any animals beyond bees, cats, one dog and two horses. This restriction also entailed an exclusively vegetarian diet. The brethren, laymen (of whom there could be as many as twenty) as well as clerks, observed a strict rule of silence, never being allowed to talk in the monastery, refectory or dormitory. The *conversi* attended Matins, Prime and Mass; after Prime they began work and compounded for the Hours they missed by genuflexions and Pater Nosters. The clerks, from the Feast of the Holy Cross until Easter, worked from Tierce until None and during this period they ate only once, after Vespers. It is difficult to know what kind of work they did since the only task mentioned is bread-making, but it is clear from the prologue to the customs that manual labour was considered to be fundamental. Only in the thirteenth century were dispensations granted: in 1216, the canons were allowed for the first time to wear shoes in winter; in 1245 they were allowed to keep cattle. Henceforth their diet included butter and cheese, but at least until the fourteenth century no-one but the sick could eat meat, this last point being in itself one of the concessions of 1245.

There is no evidence, although it has been suspected, that the canons of Hérival knew of the *Ordo Monasterii*. It was, however, through its use by certain strict communities of hermit-canons that this version of Augustine's *Rule* came into prominence at the beginning of the twelfth century. The *Ordo Monasterii* is a short document, but it is more detailed and more austere than either the *Regula Prima* or the *Regula Tertia*, the texts usually to be found under the heading *regula sancti Augustini*. It contains a clear statement of how the day is to be divided into worship, reading and manual labour, it gives strict rules on fasting and unusual liturgical instructions. As a rule, it was not kept in all its points for very long, but its appearance served to accentuate the divergent schools that had grown up within the canonical movement and thereby to cause a *crise de conscience* among the hermit-canons who were afraid they might have chosen the wrong path.

The *Ordo Monasterii* seems first to have been used at Springiersbach, an eremitical community founded in the diocese of Trier in the first decade of the twelfth century. Soon, however, the canons themselves began to wonder about the wisdom of following some of the harsher prescriptions of the rule and they consulted the pope. Gelasius told them in reply that they should abandon the liturgy of the *Ordo Monasterii* in favour of that established in the catholic church; as for manual labour and fasting, he advised them to adapt the regulations according to circumstances and the common custom of regular canons. Despite this invitation to more moderate customs, the influence of the *Ordo Monasterii* at Springiersbach was to remain strong and it made itself felt, to their unease, among other communities of hermit-canons in the vicinity. Among those concerned, for example, by the appearance of a 'new' *Rule of St Augustine* was Rolduc, in Liège. Its abbot, Richer, accordingly wrote to the canonist Raimbaud of Liège, to ask him where he could find the true canonical tradition.

Springiersbach apart, the other house to adopt the *Ordo Monasterii* was Prémontré under St Norbert: 'For although his followers claim to keep the rule of Augustine all the same if I may say so without offence to St. Augustine we see that the institution of Norbert is much more rigid and severe than that of Augustine' this was how it seemed to Herman of Laon.[1] As at Springiersbach the use of this more unusual and more demanding text gave rise to tension both within the community and among the hermit-canons who came to hear of it. In about 1124, probably because of the arrival of the Premonstratensians at Rieval, Seher, the prior and founder of the nearby Chaumouzey, wrote to St Ruf, the house which had instructed his community in the *Rule of Augustine*, to ask questions about observances. Seher's own letter has not survived but two replies he received, one from the abbot of St Ruf and the other from the bishop of Maguelonne, have and from these it is clear that it was the *Ordo Monasterii* which was troubling Seher and that he wanted reassurance that the customs he had been taught were no less authentically Augustinian than those of his new neighbours.

Prémontré, as the author of *The Orders and Callings of the Church* saw, was a leading house of a particular group of canons, to be distinguished both from the seculars who lived in towns and from the canons who lived if not among yet near men. The Premonstratensians and the canons akin to them are described by this author as living completely apart from society, as refusing to hold tithes, and as manual workers: these clearly are hermit-canons, Prémontré's place among them has not, however, always been sufficiently realised. She has too often been considered apart, and there has been much discussion about the aims of St Norbert, as to how to reconcile his preaching and his foundation, as to whether he had any fixed plans to teach his disciples. It has been felt that 'the aim [his disciples] pursued was not at first very clearly defined'.[2] But such problems arise to a large extent because historians have looked at the origins of Prémontré in the light of what she became rather than in the light of other contemporary foundations. In this context, the values of Prémontré are not 'something very different from those of other orders'[3] but, above all, an expression of the eremitical ideal. Recent research confirms this. Textual work on the customs of Arrouaise, Oigny and Prémontré have shown such similarities that it may even be that they are all based on the same (missing) text. When it was suggested to Norbert that he become abbot of St Martin, Norbert stated the terms on which he would accept. The canons subsequently refused to have him since they found his conditions revolutionary. They were those of the new hermits of the period:

'Our plan is not to seek what belongs to others, never to claim by legal pleadings or secular judges and complaints what has been taken [from us], not to bind by anathema anyone on account of any injuries or damages done to us, but on the contrary, to sum up everything briefly, I have chosen to live a fully evangelical and apostolic life in accordance with a wiser understanding.' And when he showed them the form of the evangelical way of life, how they ought to be imitators of Christ, how they ought to shun the world, how, as the voluntary poor they should bear scorn, derision and contempt and how they should tolerate hunger and thirst and nakedness and how they must follow the institutes and rules of the holy fathers they were utterly terrified both at his words and at his countenance and without hesitation they said: 'We do not want this man over us for neither our customs nor the customs of our forefathers acknowledge such a master'.[4]

The Lord did not say 'I am Custom', but 'I am Truth'. This dictum, used certainly by Urban II and probably too by Gregory VII, was implicit in the hermits' foundations, both canonical and monastic. The hermits were not only reformers, they were also revolutionaries, and as such they looked back to a golden age, to the Early Church, the *vita primitiva*. The centuries since were to them a time when the ideals of this age had been debased and forgotten; thus it mattered comparatively little whether the Carolingian rules were being well-kept, since to follow them rather than the rules of the Fathers in their earliest form was in itself something decadent and corrupt. As canons the hermits were therefore unaffected by the movement of the conservatives to restore the legislation of 817; as monks they wanted not a reformed Cluny, but the fruition of a new and radically different monastic ideal. This too was what came to be expected of them. Chalivoy, for example, was confirmed in 1138 by the lord of Boneuil on condition that if the hermits wanted to join Cîteaux or a house with similar observances they should be free to do so, if, on the other hand, they wanted to become affiliated to Cluny or a house with similar observances then his heirs would have the right to reclaim the land. Ordericus Vitalis, in describing the hermits' foundations, ended his chapter:

I have noted down for the information of posterity this account of present-day teachers, who prefer new traditions to the customs of the fathers of old, calling other monks seculars and presumptuously condemning them as violators of the Rule. I shall not abuse them, out of respect for their zeal and asceticism; nevertheless, I do not think them better than the early fathers, whose worth is proved.[5]

The differences between the new and the old monasticism have been made familiar through the conflict between Cluny and Cîteaux. What may be stressed here is that the Cistercians were not the only new monks. This may be a platitude, but it is a fact that was forgotten even by near contemporaries and later chroniclers. Because of the enormous and immediate success of the Cistercians other new monasteries were soon judged in relation to Cîteaux instead of to the new eremitical movement. This has meant that their similarities with Cîteaux – their rejection of ecclesiastical property, for example, their lay brethren, their emphasis on manual work – have been seen as a result of her influence rather than as a sign of their common eremitical origin. Robert of Torigny, for instance, wrote that Vitalis having built Savigny 'imposed on his monks modern institutions alike in some things to the Cistercians'.[6] It cannot be said that this is inaccurate but it is not far from there to the more misleading comment of a later chronicler on the foundation of Grandmont: 'these brethren follow in nearly all things the institutes of the Cistercian order...'[7] The originality of the new foundations is in this way diminished, Cîteaux herself seen out of context and larger than life.

Affligem, Tournai and Anchin as well as the better-known Fontevrault and Tiron are among the independent Benedictine houses founded by hermits, and, as far as one can tell, uninfluenced by Cîteaux. But it must be admitted that the attraction Cîteaux exercised among other eremitical houses yet remains startlingly high and in many ways difficult to explain. Individual houses and congregations both fell under her sway. To some extent, it is true, the Cistercian order increased because there was never any effective attempt to prevent it from doing so, because of its willingness to become, in the words of Professor Knowles, 'a net holding every manner of fish'.[8] Thus there is some evidence to suggest that Cîteaux was not always the hermits' first choice. Cîteaux, for example, accepted a house, Obazine, which Chartreuse, on the grounds of her size, had already rejected.

Other reasons that are often given for the Cistercian expansion are the excellence of the *Carta Caritatis* and the influence of St Bernard. Of these, the first explains the durability rather than the immediate appeal of the order for it evolved slowly and was probably unknown to most of the hermits who sought to join her. The second counted certainly with the hermits of Fountains and with Serlo of Savigny and helped the fame of the order which attracted others. Yet few eremitical sources mention Bernard by name and many were content to seek affiliation to Cîteaux or to the nearest Cistercian house rather than to Clairvaux. But Cîteaux, like Cluny, was geographically well placed to spread her gospel and she had found a *media via*, a way of life which combined the new eremitical principles with the familiarity and security of the *Benedictine Rule*. The first Cistercians had also this advantage: those who regretted their decision to go to the desert returned after a short time to Molesme. It is possible that in this way the community was spared the internal conflicts which stunted many other eremitical foundations. It is also clear that the early Cistercians were empire builders. The westward expansion of the congregation of Arrouaise, for example, was definitely and deliberately checked by ruthless Cistercian advance, a policy which for the Cistercians proved doubly rewarding. Success led to benefactions, benefactions to success. And this is a story that can be found repeated in province after province. Time and again the lion's share of donations went to the Cistercians at the expense of smaller hermitages. The hermits concerned soon found that if they could not beat the Cistercians it was better to join them. In Besançon, for example, hermits who had already become canons regular found that they would have greater security as Cistercians. In this way the foundations of Cherlieu, La Charité and Acey all passed into Cistercian hands.

Of far greater originality, constitutionally, than Cîteaux were the Italian foundations, Fonte Avellana and Camaldoli, and Chartreuse and Grandmont. The peculiarity of the first three was their closeness to the traditional concept of eremitical solitude as something personal combined with the belief of the new hermits in the complete subjection of self both to a rule and to a superior. At these foundations the hermits lived in cells either alone or with a novice. The degree of communal life at each varied but it was very much less, in all three, than in any other of the new hermits' foundations. At Fonte Avellana, the obedientiaries met for the Offices during the week; the rest of the hermits only on Sundays and certain feast days. At Camaldoli the whole community sang both the day and night offices together but not in Lent and Advent when they stayed in their cells, the hermits of Chartreuse sang only the night offices together. The emphasis at each of these communities was on contemplation and the asceticism and mortifications needed to make it possible. Fasting and silence, these were the duties of the hermit. There is a sharp contrast between these ideals and those of the hermit-hospitalers. 'We came into this desert', wrote Guy of Chartreuse, 'not to look after the bodies of others but to seek the eternal salvation of our souls'.[9]

The belief that a monk should be freed from all worldly, all Martha-like cares so that he could give his whole attention to God was carried to its extreme at Grandmont. Because of it, the hermits could not, for instance, have cattle lest they should find them engrossing, 'the greater the love you have for your cattle, the less love you will have for God'.[10] For the same reason special powers were given to the *conversi*. They were put in charge of all material and practical matters such as the distribution of food and clothing to the monks, and the monks had to accept their administration without question.

Grandmont, more than any other new foundation of the twelfth century, foreshadowed the ideals (though not the practices) of the Friars Minor. Evangelical poverty was pursued with uncompromising logic: the monks were not even to take steps to ensure that they would have enough for their own livelihood. If, as well they might, they found themselves destitute, then, with the permission of their bishop they could beg. Alone among the new hermits, but like the Friars, they were concerned not with the writings of the Fathers but solely with the precepts of the Gospel. They were themselves strongly aware of their individuality, of the revolutionary character of their house, of the demands they made on their members. They would not accept anyone under twenty, or who was physically weak or who had been a monk at another house on the grounds that the rigours of his new life, by contrast with his old, would be too much for him. They puzzled their contemporaries and they anticipated and expected their criticism. Stephen is said to have given them their reply:

> And so, brethren, many will say to you: This is a novelty you are upholding; this is neither an order nor a rule of the doctors of Holy Church. But although he who talks in this way will have the appearance and the clothing of a religious yet I tell you emphatically that he has denied the life, not knowing what is an order or a rule. Reply to him in this way: Since you criticise our life and our customs, show us why and we will gladly change our ways if your criticism can be supported by gospel authority.[11]

The *Rule of Grandmont* was to prove too radical to be satisfactory; the end of the century saw conflicts and quarrels between monks and *conversi*, and, as well, a mitigation of the early rules. 'With the passage of time', wrote Gerald of Wales, 'the dispensing advice of older and more mature men tempered the statutes which had been made at the beginning without discretion or consultation and with excessive harshness.'[12] This is not perhaps unexpected, but it must be asked what happened to the more conventional houses of hermit-monks whose schemes, because they were less ambitious, might have proved more viable.

These houses too, in the phrase Gerald of Wales used about the Cistercians, 'returned to their vomit'.[13] At Affligem, for instance, in 1092 a *conversus* entered the monastery with all his goods; in 1098 a parish was attached to the domain; by about 1119 both altars and manors were accepted. Charles Dereine has commented on these findings 'like many of the newly oriented foundations Affligem underwent a crisis and a fairly quick evolution towards the customs of traditional monasticism'.[14] The eremitical movement had managed to arouse more enthusiasm than it could sustain. It has already been mentioned that not all those who left Molesme were willing to remain at Cîteaux – over half returned with Robert. There were defections also among the first hermits of Fountains. One of the six founders of Affligem returned to the world and then tried to claim that a sixth of the property of the house belonged to him. At both Prémontré and at Tournai there was some feeling that the customs the leaders, Norbert and Odo, were trying to impose were too harsh; both these leaders, moreover, were deserted by some of their first disciples and, in the case of Odo, the total number of defections was such that after his death Amand de Castello felt it necessary to claim that the instability of certain of his disciples did not diminish Odo's sanctity. At Bec, Herluin was persuaded by Lanfranc, against his will, to enlarge the buildings of the house. His resistance is explained by Gilbert Crispin on grounds of age, 'for he was old and did not trust his failing strength',[15] but it is probable that such an account hides a rift between Lanfranc and Herluin, comparable to the conflict between Ailbert, the founder of Rolduc, and his ambitious disciple Embricon. Embricon too had pressed for larger buildings and Ailbert, rather than concede, had left to found another hermitage.

If among the first generation there were these signs, not only of misunderstanding of the eremitical ideal, but also of opposition to it, then it cannot be expected that later generations would manage better in keeping that ideal intact. In each house it is likely that 'the thing was at its best...in silence and obscurity...before the world discovered [it]'.[16] The hermits, moreover, were constantly exposed to the pressures of their friends. Bishops, eager to use the hermits in their plans for the modernisation of their dioceses, were anxious to secure their foundations and therefore endowed them whether they liked it or not. They would then give them houses of secular canons to reform despite the obvious incompatibilities of the inmates. Lay patrons, embarrassed at finding themselves in the possession of churches to which they now felt they had no right, unloaded them, willy nilly, on to the hermits. Gaucher of Aureil, for example, settled on land that belonged to the chapter of Limoges, felt bound to accept the church of Vigoulant which up to now had been in the bishop's family. Chartreuse indeed boasted that the order was never reformed because it never needed it – 'never deformed and never reformed'[17] – but then her expansion was especially and purposefully slow; only thirty-seven houses were founded in the twelfth century and the number of hermits within each remained small. Elsewhere, numbers increased, in turn more property was needed, and the outlook of the foundations altered. Charters of donations, chroniclers' comments and the measures of general chapters show, for instance, how quickly and how much the character of Cîteaux changed. The eremitical movement had given opportunities to more people to lead the religious life, it had created institutions where a new spirituality was to flourish, it had broken the monopoly of the black monks. At the same time, it had come much closer to the traditional forms of monasticism than had, in the first place, been intended. It was a movement which had proved too popular, and if this made possible its successes, it was the reason also for its failures, for the nostalgia which, by the mid-twelfth century, was felt by some of its pioneers, by those who could look back to a time when they were 'fewer in numbers, more perfect in their lives'.[18]

Appendix I

The Sources

THE first generation of hermits wrote little, or at least, little that has survived. For the second generation, however, carefully preserved records became vital. Not only were cartularies necessary for the definition and protection of properties and possessions but quite as important was the need to define and protect the collective identity of the house. Self-consciousness, born from tension and criticism, prompted the writings of many *Histories* and *Lives* at a time when there were still alive those who had known the founder and who could remember the early days.

The evaluation of this evidence is complex. In general, the most straightforward testimony comes from the cartularies. The foundation charters make it possible to pinpoint this particular turning point in the development of many communities and in a number of cases include an independent account of the beginning of the house. Charters of donation not only show the range and size of gifts acceptable to the new communities but also who were their allies and supporters during the first years.

In attempting to reconstruct the way of life of these years the least helpful sources, probably, are the later rules. In many cases the hermits had no written rules until they had relinquished their original customs in favour of those from some other eremitical house or order. Those hermits who kept their own customs, on the other hand, might not commit them to writing for many years, and it was always possible that the task of legislating might then be undertaken by someone whose ideas differed from the founder's, who was necessarily subject to different influences, and who might even be working to correct or modify customs which had proved to be impractical. Prémontré, for example, under St Norbert, followed a particularly severe form of the *Rule of Augustine* known as the *Ordo Monasterii*, but the earliest extant custumals of the house are based not on this but on the work of Norbert's successor, Hugh of Fosses. Arrouaise, a house of hermit-canons founded in the late eleventh century, gained new customs some thirty years later under Cistercian and Premonstratensian influence. However, it is true that the rules of some houses are earlier than the narrative evidence or may even supply it. The rule of Hérival composed in the mid-twelfth century by its third leader, Constantine, opens with a prologue which is the one source for the origins of the house; the *Rule of Grandmont*, according to Dom Becquet, was written shortly before the *Life* of the founder, Stephen. Yet in these cases too there must be caution. If the rule is earlier than, or as early as, the narrative source then there is reason to suspect that the latter may be coloured by the rule, and that the founder of the hermitage may be depicted living in conformity with practices invented later.

In one case, however, that of Chartreuse, it is now possible to ascertain how much of the rule to attribute to the founder, Bruno, and how much to the fifth prior, Guy, who in about 1116 wrote it down. It used to be thought that the rule accurately reflected the organisation Bruno left behind him when he was called by Pope Urban II to the curia some twenty-five years earlier. This view was seemingly supported by the description in Guibert de Nogent's autobiography, thought to have been written by him after a visit to Chartreuse in 1104, that is, only three years after the death of Bruno. Guibert's description tallies with the provisions of the rule and mentions some of the most characteristic aspects of the Carthusian system, for example, the limitation of numbers to thirteen monks. But A. de Meyer and J. M. de Smet have argued that in fact there is no evidence for the visit of 1104 and that it is much more likely that Guibert's evidence was second-hand and gained only in 1114/5, that is, in the years immediately preceding the writing of the rule by Guy. In these years Godfrey, bishop of Amiens, tried to abdicate and he retreated to Chartreuse. He was ordered back by the council of Beauvais which asked Henry, abbot of St Quentin and Hubert, one of his monks, to go to fetch him back. Guibert might then have obtained his information either from these or from the monk of Nogent whom he reported Godfrey had taken with him to Chartreuse. As for Guy's rule, Meyer and de Smet have compared it with the rule of Squillace, Bruno's Italian foundation composed by his successor Lambert, with the rule of Camaldoli, written in about 1086 by the prior Rudolph and finally with Peter Damian's rule for Fonte Avellana. Both Guy's rule and more particularly Lambert's bear a close relationship to the rules of Fonte Avellana and Camaldoli. Moreover, Lambert's rule lacks those characteristics usually regarded as specifically Carthusian. The organisation it reveals is much more similar to that of the other Italian houses than is Guy's. For example, the lower house of the laybrethren is Benedictine, as at Camaldoli, and there is no limitation of property. Bruno's own readiness to accept rich donations can be confirmed by charters. It is therefore difficult to avoid the conclusion that where there are in Guy's rule traces of Italian legislation this is Bruno's legacy; the rest, all that is most Carthusian, is of Guy's own making.

The value of the *Lives* varies greatly, depending to a large extent on when they were written, whether within a few decades of the founder's death or not for a hundred years or more. Whatever their date there is the strong probability that it was the purpose of some of the *Lives* to further the chances of the founder's canonisation, one reason for the number of miracles related, or else they were written with particular models of sanctity in mind. This does not necessarily detract from the interest of the texts. On the contrary, an examination of the miracles may show more clearly than could any apologia the nature of the hermit's priorities and concerns. By miracles, for example, the poor are fed, their cattle protected from illness and they themselves from the rapacity of their lords.

Occasionally, more than one version of a *Life* has survived: the variations, however small, are of interest. For example, there are extant two versions of the *Life* of John Gualbert. The first was written by Andrew of Strumi, probably between 1090 and 1100, the second by Atto of Vallombrosa at the beginning of the twelfth century. Atto in many passages does no more than copy Andrew but his *Life* is less than half the length. The omissions themselves tell a story. Thus Atto does not mention John's prohibition on the acceptance of chapels, for Vallombrosa in fact soon held them, nor does he give the text of a letter in which John adumbrates particularly radical views for the reform of the clergy. John has also become in Atto's *Life* a more colourless and in a sense a more respectable figure. He has become literate, he is no longer the man who could become too hungry to eat only bread and who therefore had fish specially caught.

Since the 1930s, because of the discovery of new manuscripts, the early Cistercian documents have attracted more controversy than any other monastic texts of this period. The most coherent, though by no means undisputed, arguments have been put forward by Jean Lefèvre. Here, the least pertinent are those concerned with the *Carta*

Caritatis since this was written to supply the needs of an expanding order and it therefore tells nothing of the original Cîteaux. More important is Lefèvre's discussion of the *Exordium Parvum* and the *Exordium Cistercii*, the need to know in his own words, which is 'the true account of the beginnings of Cîteaux'. It used to be held that the *Exordium Parvum* belonged to 1119, the year when Cistercian documents were first presented for papal confirmation and that the *Exordium Cistercii* was a shortened version, excluding as it does the diplomatic documents of the *Exordium Parvum*, composed for presentation to Pope Eugenius in 1152. Lefèvre, however, has argued that internal evidence makes it impossible that the *Exordium Parvum* could have been completed as early as 1119 and that the narrative account presented then was in fact the *Exordium Cistercii*. What, then, of the *Exordium Parvum*? This, he claimed, was the 1152 text and the lateness of the date explained its character. The documents it includes are commented on at some length and used to build up a picture of how much support the first Cistercians received, how their plans were officially approved, how Robert only returned to Molesme because of papal pressure. The first letter of Hugh the legate in favour of the Cistercians was inserted after the secession, whereas, according to the *Exordium Cistercii*, it was only after they had found a site that they gained papal support. A further difference between the *Exordium Cistercii* and the *Exordium Parvum* lies in the attitude to Molesme. The *Exordium Cistercii* praises life at Molesme and gives as the reason for the secession the new concept of how the *Rule* of St Benedict should be kept. The *Exordium Parvum*, on the other hand, describes Molesme as lax and in one version goes so far as to say that to have stayed there would have endangered the monks' salvation. The *Exordium Parvum* has thus all the marks of a piece of propaganda and this, according to Lefèvre, was why it was written. By 1152, the black/white monk controversy was at its height and the Cistercians were anxious to clear themselves of the charge of being merely fugitive and wilful monks.

Lefèvre's arguments breed suspicion: perhaps other accounts of new foundations, and in particular of Cistercian foundations, are similarly coloured by the quarrels of the mid-twelfth century. In general, however, it must be said that other sources lack the aggressiveness of the *Exordium Parvum* and that the accounts from those houses that became Cistercian often relate the hermits' decision to do so in terms too casual for them to be seen as official Cistercian

literature. At Silvanes and Obazine, for example, it is only after the
hermits have sought the advice of the Carthusians that they become
Cistercian. The mood is one of frank indecision as to the best course
to take rather than of conviction that to become Cistercian was
necessarily the best answer. However, when it comes to an examination of the Fountains Chronicle it would seem that we have, in the
words of Dr Baker, 'an English *Exordium*'. The chronicle includes six
letters, five from St Bernard and one from archbishop Thurstan of
York describing the secession from St Mary's for the archbishop of
Canterbury. This letter of Thurstan's, which really amounts to the
hermits' manifesto, was in the middle ages much more widely known
than the actual chronicle. It exists in two versions, a short and a long,
but neither can confidently be said to be the original, although it is
clear that the longer is the earlier. The chronicle itself, although
allegedly the reminiscences of the aged Serlo – he was nearly 100 at
the time of dictation but had joined Fountains as a young man in
1136/7 – in fact contains much derivative material. Not that this
should necessarily cause surprise or too much scepticism: possibly
there were elm trees and famines both at Clairvaux and at Fountains.
It may well be that 'many strands were used to weave and embroider
the story' but 'a synthesis of different visions and different voices' is
not necessarily our loss.

Work on Cistercian documents has tended to overshadow new
estimates of other texts belonging to the new foundations of the
eleventh and twelfth centuries. A particularly crucial reappraisal of
the texts of Grandmont has been undertaken by Jean Becquet. It used
to be held that the *Life* of Stephen had been composed by the seventh
prior, Gerard of Ithier, and was therefore both late and unreliable.
Becquet, with the help of two new manuscripts containing the *Life*,
both of them shorter than the version formerly known, has come to
the conclusion that there was in fact a *Life* before Ithier's time and
that Ithier only lengthened it by adding a new prologue, a number of
miracles and an account of Stephen's canonisation. The difficulty
then is to unravel from the rather confused chronicle evidence of who
was responsible for the original *Life*, and who for the other early
texts of Grandmont, the rule and the *Liber Sententiarum* (Book of
Maxims). The two claimants are the fourth prior, Stephen Liciac,
and Hugh of Lacerta, Stephen of Grandmont's closest disciple.
Stephen of Liciac almost certainly wrote the rule and he perhaps commissioned the *Life* and the Book of Maxims, but because of the

simple Latin of this last work Becquet is inclined to attribute it to
Hugh of Lacerta. He was clearly a layman and is said by Ithier to
have dictated memories of his master to one of the more learned
brethren. Whether the *Life* was also written down in this way or
whether it was Stephen's work is an open question, but in either case
it belongs to an earlier period, by some thirty years, than was originally thought.

There are parts of Stephen's *Life* which are nonetheless puzzling,
in particular about his early life and his stay in Italy. He is said to
have gone as a boy to Southern Italy to visit the shrine of St Nicholas
of Bari, then to have stayed twelve years with the archbishop of
Benevento, Milo. On Milo's death he lived for four years with a cardinal in Rome and then, with papal permission, set off to found a
hermitage where he might imitate the Greek hermits of Calabria
whom he had admired during his Italian stay. In 1076, he settled at
Muret. Chronologically, none of this fits together: the body of St
Nicholas was not translated from Asia Minor until 1087, Milo was
archbishop of Benevento only in 1074-5 and before then had lived in
Paris. Martène, in the eighteenth century, was therefore inclined to
dismiss much of the Italian experience, to settle Stephen in Muret
considerably later than 1076 and to make the Carthusians rather
than the Calabrians the source of his inspiration. Later historians
have generally agreed that the mention of St Nicholas in the *Life* was
a mistake, that because his shrine was much visited in the early
twelfth century it was wrongly assumed by the author that this must
have been the shrine Stephen went to see. As for the archbishop of
Benevento both Martène and Becquet accept that it was Milo although the stay could only have been for one or two years, not twelve,
and they also accept as a fact Stephen's remaining in Italy for some
years after Milo's death: thus they both reject 1076 as the starting point
for Grandmont and this is indeed why Martène can suggest the possibility of Carthusian influence. Yet 1076 is the only date the *Life* gives
and it is perhaps rash to assume that it is precisely this date which is
at fault. The inaccuracy may lie elsewhere. The author of the *Life*
more than once shows uncertainties about names: he wrongly mentions St Nicholas of Bari, he does not give the name of the cardinal
with whom Stephen stayed, nor even of the pope who approved of his
plans to become a hermit. Surely then he could have been mistaken
about the name of the archbishop. Milo would have been a name he
naturally connected with the see, just as he had connected Nicholas

with the shrine, for Milo came from France, was possibly a friend of a canon of Limoges, Humbert, to whom as archbishop he may have sent relics. If Milo is an inaccuracy then the other information presents less difficulty. Stephen could have spent twelve years in the household of an archbishop of Benevento. He could have left in 1071, a year when the see fell vacant, possibly until Milo's accession in 1074, and he still could have arrived in Muret in 1076. Chroniclers may, perhaps, be more likely to remember names than dates but the evidence in this case would seem to point to the reverse. Nor is this an exception, the chronicle of Affligem has a similar discrepancy, a date and an archbishop failing to match. The historian of the beginnings of the house, Charles Dereine, thinks it is more likely that it is the date which is correct and that the archbishop concerned with its founding was not the famous Anno of Cologne but the more obscure and therefore less memorable Sigewin.

New editions of the material for several eremitical houses have recently been completed – not only for Grandmont, but also for Arrouaise and Oigny. With the help of these texts comparative studies of customs have been made possible: Van Damme, for example, has been able to illustrate the relationship that exists between the rules of Cîteaux, Arrouaise, Oigny and Prémontré. New editions of other texts are under way and there is still manuscript material not yet fully explored. It will clearly be some time before it is possible to write a full estimate of the hermits' movement. This book has been an attempt to provide a provisional framework.

Appendix II

List of Religious Houses with Eremitical Origins

(It should not be supposed that this is a complete list. It includes only communities that have been mentioned in the text).

House	Diocese	Date of Foundation Founder(s)	Development
AFFLIGEM	Cambrai	1083 6 laymen	1086 Benedictine hospital
AGUDELLE	Saintes	c. 1116 Lambert de la Palud, disciple of Robert of Arbrissel	Benedictine Priory of Notre Dame de la Couronne (a later foundation of Lambert's)but also had to pay annual tribute to Fontevrault
ALAFOES	Viseu	1132 first mention under leader, Jean Cirita	Cistercian (Clairvaux)
ANCHIN	Cambrai	Before 1079 2 laymen	1079 Benedictine customs from Hasnon
ARROUAISE	Arras	c. 1090 2 clerks and lay hermit	Augustinian but with customs (confirmed 1139) influenced by Cistercians Double community
ARTIGE	Limoges	c. 1106 2 Venetian pilgrims	Augustinian by 1158
AUREIL	Limoges	Late eleventh century hermit-preacher Gaucher of Aureil	Augustinian customs from St Ruf 1093 consecration of church
BEC	Rouen	1034 Herluin, layman, at Bonneville	1035 Benedictine 1039 moved to Bec
BÉGARD	Tréguier	?	1130 Cistercian (L'Aumône) ceded by hermit Raoul Bégar
BÉNÉVENT	Limoges	Either 1028 or 1080	Augustinian

113

House	Diocese	Date of Foundation Founder(s)	Development
CADOUIN	Sarlat	1116 Geraud de Salles, disciple of Robert of Arbrissel	1119 Cistercian (CÎTEAUX)
CAMALDOLI	Arezzo	Early eleventh century Romuald	1085 customs drawn up by prior Rudolph
CASTERT	Liège	c. 1125 priest Bovo	1130 Augustinian priory dependent on NEUFMOUSTIER
CHAISE-DIEU	Clermont	1043 Robert, canon of Brioude	1046 Benedictine
CHALAIS	Grenoble	Early twelfth century under patronage Hugh, bp. Grenoble	Benedictine 1148 *Carta Caritatis* based on Cistercians
CHALARD	Limoges	1089 priest Geoffrey	Augustinian 1100 Consecration of church
CHALIVOY	Bourges	1133 hermit Julian	1138 Cistercian (Bouras)
LA GRANDE CHARTREUSE	Grenoble	1084 Bruno of Cologne	Customs drawn up by prior Guy c. 1116
CHAUMOUZEY	Toul	Late eleventh century hermit-priests, Athenor and Seher	Augustinian customs from St Ruf 1093 Seher blessed as abt
CHEMINON	Châlons-sur-Marne	Late eleventh century hermits in forest of Luiz	1102 Augustinian (ARROUAISE) 1109 moved from Luiz to Cheminon 1138 Cistercian (Trois-Fontaines)
CHERLIEU	Besancon	Early twelfth century group of hermits	Augustinian then 1131 Cistercian (Clairvaux)
CÎTEAUX	Châlons-sur-Saône	1198 monks from MOLESME	Head of Cistercian Order
CLAIRE-FONTAINE	Laon	1111 Ailbert of Rolduc	1126 Premonstratensian
CUXA	Elne	Late tenth century Romuald	Dispersed
DALON	Limoges	1114 Geraud de Salles	1162 Cistercian (PONTIGNY)

House	Diocese	Date of Foundation Founder(s)	Development
ÉTIVAL-EN-CHARNIE	Mans	Early twelfth century Alleaume, disciple of Bernard of TIRON	Benedictine double community 1109 consecration of church
FLÔNE	Liège	c. 1090 3 lay hermits	Augustinian by 1131 hospital
FONTAINE LES BLANCHES	Tours	c. 1125 hermits under leaderhip of Geoffrey	1134 affilitated to SAVIGNY, but secession by some of the hermits who wanted to remain independent
FONTE AVELLANA	Cagli and Pergola	977 Ludolph and Julian, disciples of Romuald	Rule written by Peter Damian, c. 1050
FONTENAY	Autun	Early twelfth century hermit Martin	1119 Cistercian (Clairvaux)
FONTEVRAULT	Poitiers	c. 1099 Robert of Arbrissel hermit-preacher	Benedictine double community
FOUNTAINS	Yorkshire	1132 monks of St Mary's, York	1134/5 Cistercian (Clairvaux)
GÂSTINES	Tours	Early twelfth century hermits	Split: some hermits became Cistercians but Augustinian community developed at Gâstines and 1138 given abbatical status
GOATHLAND	Yorkshire	Early twelfth century priest Osmund	Benedictine priory dependent on WHITBY
GRANDMONT	Limoges	1076 Stephen of Muret	Rule written by Stephen Liciac, prior 1139–63
GRANDSELVE	Toulouse	1114 Geraud de Salles	1145 Cistercian (Clairvaux)
HÉRIVAL	Toul	c. 1082 priest Engelbald	Augustinian customs by prior Constantin after 1155
JARROW	Durham	1073/4 Reinfrid, Aldwin, Aelfwig, monks, from Evesham	Benedictine
KIRKSTALL	Yorkshire	?	1147 Cistercian (Barnoldswick) ceded by hermits

House	Diocese	Date of Foundation Founder(s)	Development
KIRKSTEAD	Lincoln	?	1139 Cistercian (FOUNTAINS) ceded by hermits
LA FLÈCHE	Angers	Late eleventh century Rainaud, canon, hermit of Craon	1182 Augustinian abbey erected on Rainaud's tomb. Perhaps a new foundation
LES DUNES	Thérouanne	1107 hermit Ligerius	1138 Cistercian (Clairvaux)
LLANTHONY	St. David's	Early twelfth century hermits	Augustinian customs from Aldgate, Colchester, Merton
LORÉ	Chartres	1130 first appearance as group of hermit-preachers under leadership of Geoffrey Babion	Augustinian priory dependent on GÀSTINES
MOLESME	Langres	c. 1070 hermits in forest of Collan 1072 placed themselves under leadership of Robert, former abt of St Michel de Tonnerre	Benedictine (See also CÎTEAUX)
MONT-ST-MARTIN	Cambrai	c. 1120 Garembert, layman	1134/5 Premonstratensian double community
MONT-SALVY	St Flour	c. 1066 hermit Gausbert	Augustinian
MORIMOND	Langres	Early eleventh century hermit John	1115 Cistercian (CÎTEAUX)
NEUFMOUSTIER	Liège	1099 Peter the Hermit	Augustinian by 1179
NOSTELL	Yorkshire	Early twelfth century group of hermits	Augustinian by 1120
OBAZINE	Limoges	1130 Stephen, priest, officially confirmed as leader of group of hermits	1142 Benedictine customs from DALON 1147 Cistercian (CÎTEAUX) double community
OIGNY	Autun	Early twelfth century	Augustinian
PEBRAC	Clermont	1062 or 1079 Peter of Cahvanon, archpriest of Langeac	Augustinian
PONTIGNY	Auxerre	Early twelfth century hermit Ansius	1114 Cistercian (CÎTEAUX)

House	Diocese	Date of Foundation Founder(s)	Development
PRÉMONTRÉ	Laon	1121 Norbert, hermit-preacher, former canon of Xanten	Head of Premonstratensian Order
RADMORE	Lichfield	Before 1131 hermits on royal forest	1141 Cistercian (Bordesley) 1159 moved to Stoneleigh
REIGNY	Auxerre	Late eleventh century group of hermits	1128 Cistercian (Clairvaux)
ROLDUC	Liège	1104 Ailbert, canon of Tournai	Augustinian customs from Rottenbuch double community
ST GILLES	Liège	c. 1080 Gondran, layman	Augustinian by 1115
ST MARTIN	Tournai	1092 Odo, master of cathedral school	Augustinian then 1095 Benedictine
ST SULPICE-DES-BOIS	Rennes	Early twelfth century Raoul de la Futaie, monk of St Jouin de Marnes	Benedictine double community
SAVIGNY	Avranches	1112 Vitalis, hermit-preacher	Head of Benedictine congregation 1147 affiliated to CÎTEAUX
SAUVE-MAJEURE	Bordeaux	1080 Gerard, monk of St Peter of Corbie	Benedictine
SÈCHE-FONTAINE	Langres	c. 1082 Peter and Lambert (companions of Bruno of Cologne before the founding of LA GRANDE CHARTREUSE) on land belonging to MOLESME	Benedictine 1173 given by Molesme to Jully
SILVANES	Rodez	c. 1130 Pons de Léras, layman	1136 Cistercian (Mazan)
SPRINGIERSBACH	Triers	c. 1100 Benigne, widow	Augustinian (Ordo Monasterii) 1107 consecration of oratory
TIRON	Chartres	1109 Bernard d'Abbeville, hermit-preacher, former abt St Cyprian, Poitiers	Benedictine

House	Diocese	Date of Foundation Founder(s)	Development
VAL DI CASTRO	Camerino	c. 1000 Romuald	Benedictine 1394 united to Camaldolesian order
VALLOMBROSA	Fiesole	c. 1036 John Gualbert, monk	Benedictine
VAUCLAIR	Laon	?	1134 Cistercian (Clairvaux) ceded by hermit Robert
VICOGNE	Cambrai	c. 1125 Wido, disciple of St Norbert	Premonstratensian
WEARMOUTH	Durham	c. 1076–8 Aldwin (see JARROW)	Benedictine
WHITBY	Yorkshire	c. 1076–8 Reinfrid (see JARROW)	Benedictine

Abbreviations

Bull. Soc. Archéol. Limousin	*Bulletin de la société archéologique historique du Limousin*
MGH SS	*Monumenta Germaniae historica Scriptores* in folio
MPL	*Migne, Patrologia Latina*
RB	*Revue Bénédictine*
RHE	*Revue d'histoire ecclésiastique*
RM	*Revue Mabillon*
SCH	*Studies in Church History*

Bibliography

This is intended to cover the principal works, in English and French, of particular relevance to each chapter. For a wider bibliography the reader should consult Giles Constable, *Medieval Monasticism, A select bibliography* (University of Toronto Press, 1976).

1. INTRODUCTION

The work of David Knowles remains the best introduction to European monasticism. See in particular *From Pachomius to Ignatius, A Study in the Constitutional History of the Religious* Orders (Oxford, 1966); *The Monastic Order in England: A History of its Development from the Times of St. Dunstan to the Fourth Lateran Council* (Cambridge, 1940). Also fundamental are R. W. Southern, *The Making of the Middle Ages* (London, 1953) and *Western Society and the Church in the Middle Ages*, Pelican History of the Church, 2 (Harmondsworth, 1970). General works include C. Brooke, *The Monastic World, 1000–1300* (London, 1974) with photographs by Wim Swaan; and B. Bolton, *The Medieval Reformation* Foundations of Medieval History, (London, 1983). For a sociological approach to monasticism see Jean Séguy, 'Une sociologie des sociétés imaginées: monachisme et utopie', *Annales* XXVI (1971), 328–54. For the adoption of rules see the bibliography for Chapter 9. The twelfth-century renaissance is the subject of a very stimulating collection of essays *Renaissance and Renewal in the Twelfth Century*, R. Benson and G. Constable (eds) Oxford, 1982). See also Peter Brown, 'Society and the Supernatural', *Society and the Holy in Late Antiquity* (London, 1982), pp. 302–32. For the tenth century, K. J. Leyser, 'The tenth century condition', *Medieval Germany and its Neighbours, 900-1250* (London, 1983), pp. 1–9.

For economic change see in particular Georges Duby, *The Early Growth of the European Economy, Warriors and Peasants from C7th–C12th*, trs. H. B. Clarke (London, 1974), and also Alexander Murray, *Reason and Society in the Middle Ages*.

2. THE SHAPING OF TRADITION

The Flight to the Desert, 250–550
Both Peter Brown, *The World of Late Antiquity* (London, 1971) and Henry Chadwick, *The Early Church* Pelican History of the Church 1, (Harmondsworth, 1967) give short accounts of early monasticism. Fuller studies include Derwas Chitty, *The Desert a City* (Oxford, 1966) and Philip Rousseau, *Ascetics, Authority and the Church in the Age of Jerome and Cassian* (Oxford, 1978). There are a number of biographies: Peter Brown, *Augustine of Hippo* (London, 1967); Owen Chadwick, *John Cassian* (Cambridge, 1950); W. R. Lowther Clarke, *St. Basil the Great* (Cambridge, 1913); J. N. D. Kelly, *Jerome: His Life, Writings and Controversies* (London, 1975). Benedicta Ward has translated *The Lives of the Desert Fathers* (London, 1981) and *The Sayings of the Desert Fathers* (London, 1981). In French see A.-J. Festugière, *Les moines d'Orient*, 4 vols (Paris, 1961–5); *Antonius Magnus Eremita, 356–1956, Studia Anselmiana*, XXX-VIII (1956); *St. Martin et son temps, Studia Anselmiana*, XLVI (1961); J. Decarreaux, 'Du monachisme primitif au monachisme athonite', in *Le Millenaire du Mont Athos*,

Etudes et Mélanges 963–1963, I, (Chevetogne, 1963), pp. 19–59; L. Bouyer, *La spiritualité du Nouveau Testament et des Pères*, Histoire de la spiritualité chrétienne I (Paris, 1960). There is a great deal of literature on the *Rule of St. Benedict*, much of it concerned with the relationship between the *Rule* and the *Regula Magistri*, for example in David Knowles, *Great Historical Enterprises* (London, 1963), pp. 139–95; more to the point here is A. Hastings, 'St. Benedict and the eremitical life', *Downside Review*, LXVIII (1950), 191–211.

Monks and Hermits, 550–1150

For Grimlaicus' *Rule* and early hermits see L. Gougaud, 'Étude sur la reclusion religieuse', *RM*, X (1923), 23–39, 77–102; also J. Hubert, 'L'érémitisme et l'archeologie', in *L'Eremitismo in Occidente nei secoli XI e XII*, Miscellanea del Centro di Studi Medioevali IV (Milan, 1965), pp. 462–90. Hermits attached to Cluny are discussed by J. Leclercq, 'Pierre le Venerable et l'érémitisme clunisien', *Studia Anselmiana*, XL (1956), 99–103. Peter Brown's article 'The Rise and Function of the Holy Man in Late Antiquity', *Journal of Roman Studies*, LXI (1971), 80–101 can also be found in *Society and the Holy in Late Antiquity* (London, 1982), pp. 103–52. For Wulfric of Haselbury see Henry Mayr-Harting, 'Functions of a twelfth century recluse', *History*, LX (1975), 337–52. Christina of Markyate's *Life* has been edited and translated by C. H. Talbot, *The Life of Christina of Markyate* (Oxford, 1959). Rothma Mary Clay, *The Hermits and Anchorites of England* (London, 1914) is still useful. There is an essay on Godric on Finchale in *Benedict's Disciples*, H. Farmer (ed.) (London, 1980), pp. 195–211. The earliest vernacular song to have survived is attributed to Godric; see R. T. Davies, *Medieval English Lyrics* (London, 1963), p. 51.

Unfortunately a great deal of the literature on tenth-century monasticism is in German, but for Cluny at least a number of articles have been translated and collected in *Cluniac Monasticism in the Central Middle Ages*, Noreen Hunt (ed.) (London, 1971). This collection also contains Jean Leclercq's article 'The Monastic Crisis of the Eleventh and Twelfth Centuries', a development of Dom Morin's thesis, 'Rainaud l'Ermite et Yves de Chartres: un épisode de la crise du cénobitisme aux XIe–XIIe siècles', *RB*, XL (1928), 99–115. See also Norman F. Cantor, The Crisis of Western Monasticism 1050–1130', *American Historical Review*, LXVI (1960/I), 47–67 and D. Baker, 'Crossroads and Crises in the religious life of the late eleventh century', *SCH*, XVI (1979), 137–148. Rosalind McKitterick, *The Frankish Kingdoms under the Carolingians* (London, 1983), pp. 278–305 has a useful chapter on tenth-century monasticism, with a bibliography.

3. THE NEW HERMITS

The most important single volume for the new hermits is the collection of papers (mainly in French) *L'Eremitismo in Occidente nei secoli XI e XII*, Miscellanea del Centro di Studi Medioevali IV (Milan, 1965). In English see G. Constable, *Religious Life and Thought* (11th–12th centuries), Variorum reprints (London, 1979). On individual foundations the work of Charles Dereine, Jean Becquet and Ludo Milis is fundamental, references will be given in the order in which the foundations occur in the text. For Alice Cooke, 'A Study in the twelfth century religious revival and reform', see *Bulletin of the John Rylands Library*, IX (1925) no. 1. For pilgrimage, see Constable, *Religious Life*, pp. 3–27, (also in *Revue Historique* CCLVIII (1977), 3–27) and pp. 125–46; also J. Leclercq, 'Monachisme et pérégrination du IXe au XIIe siècle', *Studia Monastica*, III (1961), 33–52; G. B. Ladner, '*Homo Viator*: Medieval Ideas on Alienation and Order', *Speculum*, XLII (1967), 233–59; Victor and Edith Turner, *Image and Pilgrimage in Christian Culture* (New York, 1978).

For a more positive approach to the influence of Greek monasticism than is given here, see P. McNulty and B. Hamilton, '*Orientale Lumen et magistra Latinitas:* Greek influences on Western Monasticism (900–1100)', *Le Millénaire du Mont Athos 963–1963, Études et Mélanges*, I (Chevetogne, 1963), pp. 180–216. For the concept of the *vita apostolica* see C. Dereine, 'La *vita apostolica* dans l'ordre canonial du IXe au XIe siecle,' *RM*, LI (1961), 47–53; also G. Olsen, 'The idea of the *Ecclesia Primitiva* in the writings of the twelfth century canonists', *Traditio*, XXV (1969), 61–86, but above all M.-D. Chenu, *Nature, Man and Society in the Twelfth Century*, trans. by J. Taylor and L. K. Little (Chicago, 1968). The question of models is the subject of a debate between Colin Morris and C. W. Bynum. See, in the first instance, Colin Morris, *The Discovery of the Individual 1050–1200*, Church History Outlines, 5 (London, 1972) and C. W. Bynum, *Jesus as Mother: Studies in the Spirituality of the High Middle Ages*, Publications of the Centre for Medieval and Renaissance Studies, 16 (California, 1982); also C. W. Bynum 'Did the twelfth century discover the individual?' *Journal of Ecclesiastical History*, XXXI (1980), 1–17; Colin Morris, 'Individualism in Twelfth-Century Religion. Some further Reflections', ibid., 195–206.

4. THE ORIGINS AND DEVELOPMENT OF THE REGION

There is very little on Romuald in either English or French though his *Life* can be read in translation together with Bruno of Querfurt's account, *Saint Pierre Damien et Saint Bruno de Querfurt*, Textes Primitifs Camaldules, translated by L. A. Lassus (Namur, 1962). The translations are not always accurate. For Peter Damian see Jean Leclercq, *Saint Pierre Damien, Ermite et Homme d'Eglise*, Uomine e Dottrine, 8 (Rome, 1960); Robert Bultot, *Christianisme et valeurs humaines: La doctrine du mépris du monde*, IV, *Le XIe siècle*, I, *Pierre Damien* (Louvain-Paris, 1963).

There are succinct accounts of a number of hermit-leaders and their foundations, Italian and French, in Lester K. Little, *Religious Poverty and the Profit Economy in Medieval Europe* (London, 1978). For possible connections between the Italian and the French houses see D. R. Duvernay, 'Cîteaux, Vallombreuse et Etienne Harding', *Analecta Sacri Ordiris Cisterciensis*, VIII (1952), 379–494. For Artige, see J. Beequet, 'Aux origines du prieuré de l'Artige, chef d'ordre canoniale en Limousin (XIIe et XIIIe siècles)', *Bull. Soc. Archéol. Limousin*, XC (1963), 85–100. For Bénévent see Jean Becquet, 'Les chanoines réguliers de Lesterps, Bénévent et Aureil en Limonsin aux XIe et XIIe siècles, ibid., XCIX (1972), 80–135. For Herluin, see Christopher Harper-Bill, 'Herluin, Abbot of Bec and his Biographer', *SCH*, XV (1978), 15–25. For St Ruf, see C. Dereine, 'Saint-Ruf et ses coutumes aux XIe et XIIe siècles', *RB*, LIX (1949), 161–82; D. Misonion, 'La législation canoniale de Saint-Ruf d'Avignon à ses origines', *Annales du Midi*, LXXV (1963), 471–489.

Grandmont has been closely studied by Jean Becquet. Among numerous articles see 'Les institutions de l'ordre de Grandmont au moyen age', *RM*, XLII (1952), 31–42; 'La règle de Grandmont', *Bull. Soc. Archéol. Limousin*, LXXXVII (1958), 9–36; 'La première crise de l'ordre de Grandmont', ibid., LXXXVII (1960), 283–324. For the Carthusians see Bernard Bligny, 'Les premiers Chartreux et la pauvreté', *Le Moyen Age*, LVII (1951), 27–60. On the Cistercians the bibliography is vast and would be quite inappropriate here. For the problem of Cistercian sources see Appendix II; otherwise of particular interest are J. Leclercq, 'The Intentions of the Founders of the Cistercian Order', *The Cistercian Spirit: A Symposium in Memory of Thomas Merton*, Basil Pennington (ed.) (Cistercian Studies Series 3; Spencer, Mass, 1970), pp. 88–133; Louis L. Lekai, 'Ideals and Reality in Early Cistercian Life and Legislation', *Cister-*

cian Ideals and Reality, J. Sommerfeldt (ed.) (Michigan, 1978). For Prémontré see F. Petit, 'L'ordre de Prémontré de S. Norbert à Anselm d'Havelberg', *La Vita Commune del Clero nei secoli XI e XX*, I, Miscellanea del Centro di Studi Medioevali (Milan, 1962), pp. 466–471, and 'Pourquoi S. Norbert a choisi Prémontré', *Analecta Praemonstratensia*, XL (1964), 5–16; also two articles by C. Dereine, 'Les origines de Prémontré, *RHE*, XLI (1947), 352–78 and 'Le premier ordo de Prémontré, *RB*, LVIII (1948), 84–92. For Pons de Léras, see D. Baker 'Popular piety in the Lodèvois in the early twelfth century: the case of Pons de Léras', *SCH*, XV (1978), 39–47.

For the spread of the movement see L. Raison and R. Niderst, 'Le mouvement érémitique dans l'ouest de la France a la fin du XIe siècle et au debut du XIIe siècle', *Annales de Bretagne*, LV (1948), 1–46. The origins of the Cistercian houses can be checked in P. L. Janauschek, *Originum Cisterciensium* (Vienna, 1877). For Arrouaise, see Ludo Milis, *L'Ordre des Chanoines Réguliers d'Arrouaise. Son histoire et son organisation, de la fondation de l'abbaye-mère (vers 1090) à la fin des chapitres annuels (1471)*, 2 vols (Bruges, 1969). For Liège, see C. Dereine, *Les Chanoines Réguliers au Diocèse de Liège avant St. Norbert* (Louvain-Paris, 1952). The best histories of Hirsau remain in German. For England, see David Knowles, *From Pochomius to Ignatius*; and D. Baker, '"The surest road to Heaven": Ascetic Spiritualities in English Post-Conquest Religious Life', *SCH*, X (1973), 45–57 and 'The foundation of Fountains Abbey', *Northern History*, IV (1969), 29–43. For Stephen Harding's letter to Sherborne, see D. Bethell, 'An unpublished letter of St. Stephen Harding', *Downside Review*, LXXIX (1961), 349–50.

5. PROBLEMS OF ORGANISATION

Bruno's letter has been translated into French. See *Lettres des Premiers Chartreux*, I, Sources Chrétiennes, p. 88 (Paris, 1962), pp. 67–81. For Ailbert of Rolduc, see C. Dereine, *Les Chanoines Réguliers*, pp. 169–217. For Odo of Tournai, see C. Dereine, 'Odon de Tournai et la crise du cénobitisme au XIe siècles', *Revue du moyen âge latin*, IV (1948), 137–54. A great deal of work has been done on Cistercian sites, especially in England by Robert Donkin. See for example his article, 'The Site changes of Medieval Cistercian Monasteries', *Geography*, XLIV (1959), 251–8; see also G. Despy, 'Les richesses de la terre: Cîteaux et Prémontré devant l'economie de profit aux XIe et XIIe siècles', *Revue de l'Université de Bruxelles*, IV (1975), 400–23. For Silvanes, see C. H. Berman, 'The foundation and early history of the monastery of Silvanes: the economic reality', *Cistercian Ideals and Reality*, J. Sommerfeldt (ed.) (Michigan, 1978), pp. 280–318. For Affligem, see C. Dereine, 'La spiritualité "apostolique" des premiers fondateurs d'Affligem (1083–1100)', *RHE*, LIV (1959), 179–86. For Flône, see C. Dereine, *Les Chanoines Réguliers*, pp. 106–120.

For women hermits, see Jacqueline Smith, 'Robert of Arbrissel: *Procurator Mulierum*', *SCH*, Subsidia I (1978), 175–84; D. Iogna-Prat, 'La femme dans la perspective penitentielle des ermites du Bas-Maine (fin XIe début XIIe siècles), *Revue d'histoire de la spiritualité*, LIII (1977), 47–64. For devotion to the Virgin and to women saints, see Bynum, *Jesus as Mother:* pp. 136–8 and *passim*. On St Gaucher see Jean Becquet, 'La vie de Saint Gaucher, fondateur des chanoines réguliers d'Aureil en Limousin', *RM*, LIV (1964), 25–55. *I laici nella 'Societas christiana' dei secoli XI e XII*, Miscellanea del Centro di studi medioevali 5 (Milan, 1968) contains articles on both the laity and women.

6. OBSERVANCES

For poverty see the important collection of papers, *Études sur l'histoire de la pauvreté*, M. Mollat (ed.), 2 vols (Paris, 1974); also Lester K. Little, *Religious Poverty and the Profit Economy*. For the particular problem of tithes, see G. Constable, *Monastic Tithes from their Origins to the Twelfth Century*, Cambridge Studies in Medieval Life and Thought, x (Cambridge, 1964). For charitable work, see J. M. Bienvenu, 'Pauvreté, misères et charité en Anjou aux XIe et XIIe siècles', *Moyen Age*, LXXII (1966), 387–424; LXXIII (1967), 5–33, 189–216. For the liturgy see Chrysogonous Waddell, 'The early Cistercian experience of liturgy', *Rule and Life: an Interdisciplinary Symposium*, M. Basil Pennington (ed.) (Cistercian Studies Series 12; Spencer, Mass. 1971) pp. 77–115 and 'The reform of the liturgy from a renaissance perspective', *Renaissance and Renewal*, pp. 37–67. For the manual attributed to Gualbert, see A. Wilmart, 'Le Manuel de prières de S. Jean Gualbert', *RB*, XLVIII (1936), 259–99. For the significance of food and clothes, see Albert d'Haenens 'Quotidienneté et contexte: pour un modèle d'interpretation de la realité monastique medievale (XIe–XIIe siecles)', Miscellanea del Centro di Studi Medioevali IX (1980), pp. 567–97.

7. HERMITS, REFORM AND PREACHING

For a bibliography on the Gregorian Reform and a different view from the one given here, see H. E. J. Cowdrey, *The Cluniacs and the Gregorian Reform* (Oxford, 1970). For heresy see *Hérésies et Sociétés dans l'Europe pre-industrielle IIe–18e siècles*, J. le Goff (ed.), Civilisations et sociétés x (Paris, 1968); R. I. Moore, *The Origins of European Dissent* (London, 1977) and 'Some heretical attitudes to the Renewal of the Church', *SCH*, XIV (1977), 87–93; J. Musy, 'Mouvements populaires et heresies au XIe siècle en France', *Revue Historique*, CCLIII (1975), 33–76; C. Brooke, 'Heresy and Religious Sentiment 1000–1250', *Medieval Church and Society* (New York, 1972), pp. 139–61; Janet Nelson, 'Society, theodicy and the origins of heresy: towards a reassessment of the medieval evidence', *SCH*, IX (1972), 65–77.

For preaching, see Michel Zink, *La prédication en Langue romane avant 1300* (Paris, 1976); Colin Morris 'A critique of popular religion: Guibert of Nogent: *The Relics of the Saints*', *SCH*, VIII (1972), 65–77; Barbara H. Rosenwein and Lester K. Little, 'Social Meaning in the Monastic and Mendicant Spiritualities', *Past and Present*, LXIII (1974), 4–32; R. I. Moore, 'Family, Community and Cult on the Eve of the Gregorian Reform', *Transactions of the Royal Historical Society* 5th Series, XXX (1980), 49–69.

8. REACTIONS TO HERMITS

It is not possible to suggest any reading (beyond works referred to in the notes) which does not focus on the controversies in a more developed form than is appropriate here (for example, see David Knowles, 'Cistercians and Cluniacs: the controversy between St. Bernard and Peter the Venerable', *The Historian and Character and Other Essays* (Cambridge, 1963), pp. 50–75).

9. THE ADOPTION OF AN ORDER AND CUSTOMS

For work on canons regular C. Dereine leads the field. A list of his numerous articles
may be found in the bibliography of *Les Chanoines Réguliers*. Other more recent
studies which show the hermits' role include Jean Becquet, 'Les Chanoines Réguliers
du Chalard (Haute-Vienne)', *Bull. Soc. Archéol. Limousin*, XCVIII (1971), 153–72;
Rene Locatelli, 'Les chanoines et la reforme dans le diocese de Besancon', *Cahiers
d'histoire* (1975) 704–18; J. Chatillon, 'La crise de l'église aux XIe et XIIe siècles et les
origines des grands federations canoniales', *Revue d'histoire de la spiritualité*, LIII
(1977), 3–45; Ludo Milis, 'Ermites et Chanoines réguliers au XII siècle', *Cahiers de
civilisation médiévale*, XXII (1979), 39–80; M. Parisse, 'Les chanoines réguliers en
Lorraine. Fondations, expansion (XIe–XIIe siècles)', *Annales de l'Est*, XX (1968),
347–88. See also *La vita commune del clero nei secoli XI e XII. Atti della settimana
di studio, Mendola, settembre 1959*, 2 vols, Miscellanea del Centro di studi
Medioevali, 3 (Milan, 1962).

For a study of the relationship between rules see J.-B. Van Damme, 'La "Summa
Cartae Caritatis" Source de Constitutions Canoniales', *Cîteaux Commentarii Cisterciensis* (1972), 5–54.

10. THE END OF THE HERMITAGES

For Hérival, see A. Galli, 'Les origines du prieuré de Notre-Dame d'Hérival', *RM*,
XLIX (1959), 1–34. For the *Ordo Monasterii*, see C. Dereine, 'Les coutumiers de Saint-
Quentin de Beauvais et de Springiersbach', *RHE*, XLI (1946), 411–42; 'Le premier *or-
do* de Prémontré', *RB*, LVIII (1948), 84–92.

APPENDIX I

For the sources for Grandmont see J. Becquet, 'Les premiers écrivains de l'ordre de
Grandmont', *RM*, XLIII (1953), 121–37; 'S. Etienne de Muret et l'archeveque de
Bénévent, Milon', *Bull. Soc. Archéol. Limousin*, LXXXVI (1957), 403–9. On early
Carthusian development see A. de Meyer and J. M. de Smet, 'Notes sur quelques
sources littéraires relatives à Guigue Ier, cinquième prieur de la Grande-Chartreuse',
RHE, XLVIII (1953), 168–95. For the lives of Robert of Molesme see J. Lèfevre, 'Saint
Robert de Molesme dans l'opinion monastique du XIIe et du XIIIe siècle', *Analecta
Bollandiana*, LXXIV (1956), 75–80. For criticism of Lefèvre's work on Cistercian
documents see D. Knowles, 'The primitive Cistercian documents' in *Great Historical
Enterprises* (London, 1963), pp. 197–224. Other articles written against Lefèvre's
work include J. Winandy, 'Les origines de Cîteaux et les travaux de M. Lefèvre', *RB*,
LXVII (1957), 49–76; J. B. Van Damme, 'Autour des origines cisterciennes', *Collec-
tanea ordinis Cisterciensium Reformatorum*, XX (1958), 56–168, 379–90. The debate
is by no means closed: for Fountains, see Derek Baker, 'the genesis of English Cistercian Chronicles', *Analecta Cisterciensia*, XXV (1969), 14–41; XXXI (1975), 179–212.

It will be clear from the notes that most sources are still to be found in Migne,
Patrologiae Latina and the *Monumenta Germaniae Historica Scriptores*. Notable exceptions are Peter Damian's *Vita b. Romualdi* G. Tabacco (ed.), *Fonti per la storia
d'Italia*, XCIV (Rome, 1957); the documents for Grandmont, Jean Becquet (ed.), *Corpus Christianorum, Continuatio Mediaevalis*, VIII (Turnhout, 1968) and the *Constitu-
tiones Canonicorum Regularium Ordinis Arroasiensis*, L. Milis and J. Becquet (eds),
Corpus Christianorum, Continuatio Mediaevalis XX (Turnhout, 1970).

References

These are references only to actual quotations. For other references, consult the bibliography.

—

1. INTRODUCTION

1. Richard Cobb, *Times Literary Supplement*, 25 December 1981, p. 1483.
2. Peter Damian, *Vita Romualdi*, G. Tabacco (ed.), *Fonti per la storia d'Italia*, XCIV (Rome, 1957), Ch. 37, p. 78.
3. Louis MacNeice, *The Dark Tower* (London, 1964), p. 35.
4. Ordericus Vitalis, *Historia Ecclesiastica*, M. Chibnall (ed.), Nelson's Medieval Texts (Oxford, 1973), Bk. VIII, Ch. 26, p. 310.
5. D. Knowles, *From Pachomius to Ignatius, A Study in the Constitutional History of the Religious Orders* (Oxford, 1966), p. 16.
6. Brenda Bolton, *The Medieval Reformation*, Foundations in Medieval History (London, 1983), p. 36. Cf. C. Brooke, *The Monastic World* (London, 1974), p. 80.
7. The phrase is Le Goff's, cited in P. Brown, 'Society and the Supernatural: A Medieval Change', *Society and the Holy in Late Antiquity*, (London, 1982), p. 302, n. 1.
8. Ordericus Vitalis, Bk. X, pp. 295–6.
9. H. Peltier, 'Hugues de Fouilloy chanoine régulier, prieur de Saint-Laurent-au-Bois', *Revue du moyen age latin*, II (1946), 32.
10. Caroline Walker Bynum, 'Did the Twelfth Century Discover the Individual?', *Journal of Ecclesiastical History*, XXXI (1980), 16.
11. Cited by Gerhart B. Ladner, 'Terms and Ideas of Renewal', *Renaissance and Renewal in the Twelfth Century*, R. Benson and Giles Constable (eds) (Oxford, 1982), p. 6.
12. Giles Constable, 'Renewal and Reform in Religious Life', *Renaissance and Renewal*, pp. 38–9.
13. Ailred of Rievaulx, cited in D. Knowles, *The Monastic Order in England, 943–1216* (Cambridge, 1949), p. 221.
14. R. W. Southern, *Western Society and the Church in the Middle Ages*, Pelican History of the Church, 2 (Harmondsworth, 1970), pp. 255–6.
15. *Anglo-Saxon Chronicle*, 1085, G. N. Garmonsway (ed.), Everyman edn (London, 1953), p. 216.
16. G. Duby, *La Vita commune del clero nei secoli XI e XII*, Miscellanea del Centro di studi medioevali III (1962), p. 73.
17. Cited in A. Murray, *Reason and Society in the Middle Ages* (Oxford, 1978), p. 73.
18. Lester K. Little, *Religious Poverty and the Profit Economy in Medieval Europe* (London, 1978), p. 70.
19. Janet Nelson, 'Society, Theodicy and the origins of Heresy', *SCH*, IX (1972), 73.

2. THE SHAPING OF TRADITION

1. Athanasius, *Vita S. Antonii*, Ch. 14, Migne, *Patrologiae Graeca*, XXVI, col. 866.

2. A. Momigliano, 'Christianity and the decline of the Roman Empire', in *The Conflict between Paganism and Christianity in the Fourth Century*, A. Momigliano (ed.), Oxford Warburg Studies (Oxford, 1963), p. 11.

3. *Regulae Fusius Tractatae*, Migne, *Patrologiae Graeca*, XXXI, col. 930.

4. Ibid., col. 934.

5. Augustine, *Confessiones*, Bk. VIII, Ch. 12, *MPL*, XXXII, col. 762.

6. *Ep.* 125, *Select Letters of St. Jerome*, F. A. Wright (ed.), Loeb Classical Library (London, 1954) text and translation, pp. 412–15.

7. Cassian, *Conlationes*, XVIII, 6, E. Pichery (ed.), Sources Chrétiennes LXIV (Paris, 1959), pp. 16–17.

8. *Conlationes*, XVIII, 11, p. 22.

9. *Conlationes*, XVIII, 4, p. 14.

10. *Conlationes*, XIX, 10, p. 48.

11. *Conlationes*, XIX, 8, p. 46.

12. *Conlationes*, XIX, 9, p. 47.

13. Cassiodorus, *Institutiones*, R. A. B. Mynors (ed.) (Oxford, 1937), p. 74.

14. *The Rule of St. Benedict*, Ch. 1, p. 14. The edition and translation used throughout is that of J. McCann (London, 1952).

15. Ibid., p. 16.

16. Ibid., Ch. 73, p. 162.

17. Ibid., prologue, p. 12.

18. Ibid., Ch. 73, p. 160.

19. Ibid.

20. Ibid., Ch. 1, p. 14.

21. *Commentaria in Regulam S. Benedicti*, *MPL*, CII, col. 725.

22. Ibid., col. 728.

23. *Regula Solitarium*, Ch. 23, *MPL*, CIII, col. 604.

24. *Vitae Patrum seu Liber de vita quorundam feliciosorum*, Ch. 12, *MPL*, LXXI.

25. Bede, *Life of Cuthbert*, B. Colgrave (ed.), *Two Lives of St. Cuthbert* (Cambridge, 1940), Ch. XXII, p. 228.

26. Peter Brown, 'The rise and function of the Holy Man in Late Antiquity', *Journal of Roman Studies*, LXI (1971), 93; also in *Society and the Holy in Late Antiquity* (London, 1982), pp. 103–52.

27. Henry Mayr-Harting, 'Functions of a twelfth century recluse', *History*, LX (1975), 344–5.

28. C. J. Holdsworth, 'Christina of Markyate', *SCH*, Subsidia I (Cambridge, 1978), 203.

29. Rimbert, *Vita Anskarii*, Ch. 35, G. Waitz (ed.), *Monumenta Germaniae historica Scriptores Rerum Germanicarum in usum scholarum* (Hanover, 1884), p. 66.

30. *Vita S. Mederici abb. Aeduensis*, *Acta Sanctorum Ordinis S. Benedicti*, III, i, p. 12.

31. *The Life of Christina of Markyate*, ed. and trans. C. H. Talbot (Oxford, 1959), p. 81.

32. *Gesta Abbatum Fontenellensium*, Ch. 4, S. Loewenfeld (ed.), *Monumenta Germaniae historica Scriptores Rerum Germanicarum in usum scholarum* (Hanover, 1886), p. 21.

33. This much used phrase was coined by Dom Morin, 'Rainaud l'ermite et Ives de Chartres: un épisode de la crise du cénobitisme aux XI–XII siècles', *RB*, XL (1928), 99–115.

34. John of Salerno, *Vita Odonis*, *MPL*, CXXXIII, Bk. I, Ch. 22, col. 53.

35. R. W. Southern, *The Making of the Middle Ages* (London, 1953), p. 161.

3. THE NEW HERMITS

1. Morin, 'Rainaud l'ermite ...', p. 112.

2. J. Leclercq, *L'Eremitismo in Occidente nei secoli XI e XII*, Miscellanea del centro di studi medioevali IV (Milan, 1965), p. 594.

3. Ibid.

4. J. Leclercq and J. P. Bonnes, *Un Maître de la Vie Spirituelle au XIe Siècle* (Paris, 1946), pp. 21–2.

5. *Rule of Benedict*, Ch. 1, p. 15.

6. Herman, *Liber III de Miraculis S. Mariae Laudunensis*, Ch. 3, *MGH SS*, XII, p. 656.

7. Giraldus Cambrensis; cited W. Davies, *Wales in the Early Middle Ages* (Leicester, 1982), p. 153.

8. Herman, *Liber de Restauratione Monasteri S. Martini Tornacensis*, Ch. 39, *MGH SS*, XIV, p. 29.

9. *Magna Vita S. Hugonis*, D. Douie and H. Farmer (eds), Nelson's Medieval Texts (Edinburgh etc., 1961–2), 1, p. 23.

10. Edward Peters, *Heresy and Authority in Western Europe* (London, 1980), pp. 60–1.

11. C. Dereine, 'Les coutumiers de Saint-Quentin de Beauvais et de Springiersbach', *RHE*, XLIII (1948), 440.

12. *Vita Stephani Obazinensis*, ed., with a French translation, by M. Aubrun, Institut d'Études du Massif Central, fasc. VI (Clermont-Ferrand, 1970), Bk. I, Ch. 7, p. 54.

13. *Lettres des premiers Chartreux*, un Chatreux (ed.), Sources Chrétiennes, LXXXVIII (Paris, 1962), I, p. 70.

14. Cited in C. Brooke, *The Monastic World* (London, 1974), pp. 78–9.

15. Seher, *Primordia Calmosiacensia*, Bk. I, *MGH SS*, XII, p. 326.

16. Serlo, *Memorials of the Abbey of St. Mary of Fountains*, J. R. Walbran (ed.), Surtees Society, XLII (1863), I, p. 35.

17. Ordericus Vitalis, *Historica Ecclesiastica*, Bk. VIII, ed. and trans. by M. Chibnall, Oxford Medieval Texts (Oxford, 1973), p. 333.

18. *Vita Stephani Obazinensis*, Bk. I, Ch. 3, p. 48.

19. *Vita domni Herluini Abbatis Beccensis*, J. Armitage Robinson (ed.), *Gilbert Crispin Abbot of Westminster* (Cambridge, 1911), p. 87.

20. Brenda Bolton, '*Paupertas Christi*: old wealth and new poverty in the twelfth century', *SCH*, XIV, 100.

21. V. W. Turner, *The Ritual Process* (Harmondsworth, 1969), pp. 95–6.

22. Hugh the Frenchman, *Tractatus de Conversione Pontii de Larazio et Exordio Salvaniensis Monasterii Vera Narratio*, Ch. II, E. Baluze (ed.), *Miscellania* (Lucques, 1761), p. 182.

23. William of St. Thierry, *Epistola ad Fratres de Monte-Dei*, M. Davy (ed.) (Paris, 1940), p. 70.

24. *Lettres des premiers Chartreux*, I, p. 74.

25. Morin (ed.), 'Rainaud l'ermite ...', p. 101.

26. *Vita Norberti archiepiscopi Magdeburgensis*, Ch. 12, *MGH SS*, XII, p. 684.

27. Vetera Hyreevallis Statuta, C. L. Hugo (ed.), *Monumenta Sacrae Antiquitatis* (Etival, 1725), I, p. 136.

28. Serlo, *Memorials of ... Fountains*, p. 13.

29. Cited in R. W. Southern, *Western Society and the Church in the Middle Ages*, Pelican History of the Church, 2 (Harmondsworth, 1970), p. 251.

30. *Regula Stephani*, J. Becquet (ed.), Corpus Christianorum, Continuatio Mediaevalis VIII (Turnhout, 1968), p. 66.

31. *Vita Norberti*, Ch. 12, p. 683.

4. THE ORIGINS AND DEVELOPMENT OF THE MOVEMENT

1. Peter Damian, *Op.* XV, Ch. 1, *MPL*, CXLV, col. 336–7.
2. Peter Damian, *Vita beati Romualdi*, Ch. 4, G. Tabacco (ed.), *Fonti per la storia d'Italia* (Rome, 1957), pp. 20–1.
3. Ibid., Ch. 37, p. 78.
4. Ibid., Ch. 24, p. 51.
5. Bruno of Querfurt, *Vita Quinque Fratrum, MGH SS*, XV, ii, Ch. 2, p. 718.
6. Marbod of Rennes, *Vita sancti Roberti abbatis Casae Dei, MPL*, CLXXI, Ch. 7, col. 1509).
7. For what follows, see D. Baker, 'The surest road to heaven', *SCH*, X, 51.

5. PROBLEMS OF ORGANISATION

1. Eadmer, *Vita S. Anselmi*, R. W. Southern (ed.), Nelson's Medieval Texts (Edinburgh etc., 1962), p. 10.
2. *Vita ... Roberti ... Casae Dei, MPL*, CLXXI, Ch. 8, col. 1509–10.
3. Hugh the Frenchman, *Tractatus de Conversione Pontii de Larazio et Exordio Salvaniensis Monesterii Vera Narratio*, Ch. II, E. Baluze (ed.), *Miscellania* (Lucques, 1761), p. 182.
4. Albert d'Haenens, 'Quotidienneté et contexte', Miscellanea del Centro di Studi Medioevali, IX (Milan, 1980), p. 595.
5. *Exordium seu fundatio monasterii Haffligeniensis*, Ch. 2, V. Coosemans and C. Coppens (eds), Affligemensia, IV (1947), p. 14.
6. *Vita ... Roberti ... Casae Dei*, Ch. II, col. 1510.
7. *Vita Stephani ... Obazinensis*, Bk. 1, Ch. 5, p. 52.
8. Baudry of Dol, *Vita b. Roberti de Arbrisello, MPL*, CLXII, col. 1052.
9. V. W. Turner, *The Forest of Symbols* (Cornell University Press, 1967), p. 110.
10. *Vita b. Gaufredi ... (Casteliensis)*, A. Bosvieux (ed.), *Mémoires de la Société des sciences naturelles et archéologiques de la Creuse*, III, (1862), Bk. 1, Ch. 6, p. 101.
11. *Vita Stephani ... Obazinensis*, Bk. 1, Ch. 16, p. 70.
12. Seher, *Primordia Calmosiacensia*, Bk. 1, p. 326.
13. *Vita Stephani ... Obazinensis*, Bk. 1, Ch. 17, p. 70.
14. *Liber de Restauratione S. Martini Tornacensis*, Ch. 70, p. 307.
15. Cited in D. Meade, 'From turmoil to solidarity', *American Benedictine Review*, XIX(1968), 339.
16. *Bernold of Constance, MGH SS*, V, col. 452–3.
17. *Vita Romualdi*, Ch. 64, p. 105.
18. *Vita Johannis*, Ch. 21, p. 1085.
19. M.-D. Chenu, *Nature, Man and Society in the Twelfth Century*, trans. Taylor and Little (Chicago, 1968), p. 219.
20. *Vita Stephani ... Obazinensis*, Bk. II, Ch. 2.
21. *Tractatus de conversione Pontii de Larazio*, Ch. 24, p. 184.
22. Cited in C. Morris, 'Equestris Ordo: Chivalry as a vocation in the twelfth century', *SCH*, XV (1978), 88.
23. Ibid.
24. Baudry of Dol, *Vita b. Roberti*, Ch. 3, 19, col. 1053.
25. 'Vie de Gaucher d'Aûreil', J. Becquet (ed.), *RM*, LIV (1964), Ch. 12, p. 52.
26. Ibid.
27. *Vita Stephani ... Obazinensis*, Bk. II, Ch. 47, p. 170.
28. J. Leclercq, *Monks and Love in Twelfth Century France* (Oxford, 1979), p. 23.
29. Caroline Walker Bynum, *Jesus as Mother, Studies in the Spirituality of the High Middle Ages* (California, 1982), p. 146.

6. OBSERVANCES

1. *Vita Stephani ... Obazinensis*, Bk. 1, Ch. 2, p. 46.

2. C. Dereine, *Les Chanoines Réguliers au Diocese de Liège avant St. Norbert* (Louvain-Paris, 1952), p. 108, n. 4.

3. *Memorials of ... Fountains*, p. 23.

4. Morin, 'Rainaud l'ermite ...', p. 101.

5. *Vita archiepiscopi Magdeburgensis, MGH SS*, XII, *Norberti*, Ch. 9, p. 678.

6. *Vita Johannis*, Ch. 15. p. 1084.

7. *Liber Sententiarum*, J. Becquet (ed.), *Corpus Christianorum Continuatiu Mediacualis*, VIII (Turnhout, 1968), Bk. 1, p. 6.

8. Ibid.

9. *Exordium Cisterciensis coenobii*, J. Turk (ed.), *Cistercii Statuta Antiquissima, Analecta sacra ordinis cisterciensis*, IV (1948), p. 33.

10. Cited in G. Constable, *Monastic tithes from their origins to the twelfth century* (Cambridge, 1964), p. 137.

11. R. I. Moore 'Family, community and cult on the Eve of the Gregorian Reform', *Transactions of the Royal Historical Society*, 5th series, XXX (1980), pp. 54-5.

12. *Vita Bernardi, MPL*, CLXXII, col. 1384. For this extract in translation, Rosalind Brooke, *The Coming of the Friars*, Historical Problems: Studies and Documents (London, 1975), p. 50.

13. For Gerhoh of Reichersberg see Lester K. Little, *Religious Poverty and the Profit Economy in medieval Europe*, pp. 110–112.

14. *Liber de Restauratione S. Martini Tornacensis*, Ch. 68, p. 306.

15. 'Monachorum Afflighemeniensium et imprimis b. Fulgentii primi coenobii abbatis statutum de decimis rerum omnium in eleemosynas expendendis', H. P. Vanderspeeten (ed.), *Analecta Bollandiana*, IV (1885), p. 254.

16. Rupert of Deutz, *In quaedam capitula regula S. Benedicti, MPL*, CLXX, col. 517.

17. *Annales Rodenses*, p. 692.

18. C. Dereine (ed.), 'Les coutumiers de Saint-Quentin de Beauvais et de Springiersbach', *RHE*, XLIII (1948), 437.

19. Cited in C. Dumont, 'Humanism and rusticity: aim and practice of the early Cistercians', *Cistercian Studies*, XVII (1982), 68.

20. Jacques Le Goff, *Time, Work and Culture in the Middle Ages*, trans. A. Goldhammer (Chicago, 1980), p. 115.

21. Ibid.

22. For what follows, *Libellus de Diversis Ordinibus et Professionibus qui sunt in Aecclesia*, G. Constable and B. Smith (eds), Oxford Medieval Texts (Oxford, 1972), pp. 66–72.

23. G. Duby, 'The Culture of the Knightly Class: Audience and Patronage', *Renaissance and Renewal*, pp. 250–1.

24. *Tractatus de Conversione Pontii de Larazio*, Ch. 16, p. 182.

25. *Libellus de Diversis Ordinibus et Professionibus*, p. 66.

26. *Rule of Grandmont*, J. Becquet (ed.), *Corpus Christianorum continuatio mediaevalis*, VIII (Turhout, 1968), Ch. XXXVII, p. 86.

27. *Liber de Restauratione S. Martini*, Ch. 68, p. 306.

28. C. Morris, *The Christian World*, G. Barraclough (ed.) (London, 1981), p. 142.

29. *Vita Stephani ... Obazinensis*, Bk. 11, Ch. 13, p. 114.

30. Andrew, *Vita altera Roberti*, Ch. 6, *MPL*, CLXII, col. 1073.

31. *Vita Stephani ... Obazinensis*, Bk. 1, Ch. 22, p. 76.

32. *Vita Romualdi*, Ch. 9, p. 31.

33. *Vita Stephani ... Obazinensis*, Bk. I, Ch. 18, p. 72.

34. 'Inédits de S. Pierre Damien', J. Leclercq (ed.), *RB*, LXVII (1957), p. 158.
35. R. W. Southern, *The Making of the Middle Ages*, p. 228.
36. Albert d'Haenens, 'Quotidienneté et contexte', p. 576.
37. Ordericus Vitalis, *Historia Ecclesiastica*, Bk. VIII, pp. 312–26.
38. Ibid., p. 312.
39. Marbod of Rennes, *Ep.* VI, *MPL*, CLXXI, col. 1483.
40. Mary Douglas, *Natural Symbols* (London, 1970), p. 102.

7. HERMITS, REFORM AND PREACHING

1. Lampert of Hersfeld, *Annales*, O. Holder-Egger (ed.), *SRG* (Hanover and Leipzig, 1894), p. 277.
2. *Vita Romualdi*, Ch. 35, p. 75.
3. *Vita Johannis*, Ch. 75, *MGH SS*, XXX ii, p. 1098. Cited in C. Morris, '*Iudicium Dei*: the social and political significance of the duel in the eleventh century', *SCH*, XII (1975), 106.
4. *Vita Norberti*, Ch. 7, p. 676.
5. F. Petit, *La Spiritualite des Prémontrés* (Paris, 1947), p. 274.
6. *Ep.* 365, *MPL*, CLXXXII, col. 570.
7. *Vita Norberti*, Ch. 4, p. 673.
8. *Vita Bernardi*, Ch. 7, col. 1403.
9. Ibid., Ch. 6, col. 1397.
10. Ordericus Vitalis, *Historia Ecclesiastica*, p. 332.
11. *Tractatus de conversione Pontii de Larazio*, Ch. 12, p. 182.

8. REACTIONS TO HERMITS

1. *Ep.* 37, *MPL*, CLXII, col. 50.
2. *Ep.* 192, *MPL*, CLXII, col. 201.
3. Cited in H. M. Colvin, *The White Canons in England* (Oxford, 1951), p. 3.
4. Cited in C. Dereine, 'La spiritualité "apostolique" des premiers fondateurs d'Affligem', p. 63.
5. *Tractatus de conversione Pontii de Larazio*, Ch. 18, p. 183.
6. H. Peltier, 'Hugues de Fouilloy, chanoine régulier, prieur de Saint-Laurent-au-Bois', *Revue du moyen âge latin*, II (1946), 29.
7. *Vita Johannis*, Ch. 45, pp. 1089–90.
8. *Magna Vita Sancti Hugonis* Vol. 1, D. Douie and H. Farmer (eds), Nelson's Medieval Texts (Edinburgh, 1961), p. 81.
9. Ordericus Vitalis, *Historia Ecclesiastica*, Bk. VIII, p. 313.
10. J. Leclercq, 'Le poème de Payen Bolotin contre les faux ermites', *RB*, LXVIII, 81.
11. *Libellus de Diversis Ordinibus*, p. 99.
12. Ibid., p. 29.
13. Ibid., p. 67.
14. Beryl Smalley, 'Ecclesiastical attitudes to Novelty, c. 1100–1250', *Studies in Medieval Thought and Learning* (London, 1981), p. 103.
15. Ibid., p. 107.
16. Cited in G. Constable, 'Renewal and Reform in Religious Life', p. 65.

9. THE ADOPTION OF AN ORDER AND CUSTOMS

1. *Vita Stephani ... Obazinensis*, Bk. 11, Ch. 1, p. 96.
2. Peregrinus, *Historia Praelatorum et possessionum ecclesiae b. Mariae de Fontanis*, L. d'Achéry (ed.), *Spicilegium*, II (Paris, 1723), Ch. 6, pp. 574–5.
3. Hugh of St. Victor; cited in C. W. Bynum 'The discovery of the individual', p. 10.
4. *Memorials of ... Fountains*, p. 35.
5. The debate is given in J. Dickinson, *The Origins of the Austin Canons and their Introduction into England* (London, 1950), p. 30.
6. *Vita Romualdi*, Ch. 35, pp. 75–6.
7. *Vita Johannis*, Ch. 29, p. 1087.
8. Seher, *Primordia Calmosiacensia*, Bk. I, p. 326.
9. *Tractatus de conversione Pontii de Larazio*, Ch. 20, p. 183.
10. *Exordium ... Haffligeniensis*, Ch. 5, p. 15.
11. *Vita Stephani ... Obazinensis*, Bk. 11, Ch. 1, p. 96.
12. 'Vie de Gaucher d'Aureil', Ch. 13, p. 52.
13. Herman, *Liber de Restauratione ... S. Martini Tornacensis*, Ch. 4, p. 277.
14. *Vita Stephani ... Obazinensis*, Bk. I, Ch. 26, p. 82.
15. Ibid.
16. Ibid., Bk. 11, Ch. 7, p. 106.
17. Anselm of Havelberg, *De Unitate fidei et Multiformitate Vivendi ab Abel Justo usque ad Novissimum Electum, MPL*, CLXXXVIII, col. 1141.

10. THE END OF THE HERMITAGES

1. *Liber III de Miraculis b. Mariae Laudunensis*, Ch. 7, p. 659.
2. A. Fliche, *Du Premier Concile du Lateran à l'avenement d'Innocent III* (1123–1198), Histoire de l'Eglise IX (Paris, 1948), p. 127.
3. Ibid.
4. *Vita Norberti*, Ch. 9, pp. 678–9.
5. Ordericus Vitalis, *Historia Ecclesiastica*, Bk. VIII, Ch. 27, pp. 332–3.
6. Robert of Torigny, *Tractatus de Immutatione Ordinis Monachorum, MPL*, CCII, col. 1312.
7. *Chronica S. Bertini, MGH SS*, XXV, p. 784.
8. D. Knowles, *The Monastic Order in England* (Cambridge, 1950), p. 218.
9. *Consuetudines, MPL*, CIII, Ch. 20, col. 674–5.
10. *Regula S. Stephani*, Ch. 7, p. 74.
11. *Liber Sententiarum, conclusio*, p. 60.
12. Gerald of Wales, *Speculum Ecclesiae*, III, Ch. 21 in *Opera*, J. S. Brewer, J. F. Dimock and G. F. Warner (eds), Rolls Series (London, 1861–91), IV, p. 256.
13. Ibid.
14. C. Dereine, 'La spiritualité "apostolique" des premiers fondateurs d'Affligem', p. 65.
15. *Vita Herluini*, p. 98.
16. D. Knowles, *The Monastic Order*, p. 223.
17. For the history of this phrase see A. King, *Liturgies of the Religious Orders* (London, 1955), pp. 1–2.
18. *Vita Stephani ... Obazinensis*, Bk. 1, Ch. 16, p. 70.

Index